My STAR READER

Grade 4

Table of Contents

Realistic Fiction 2

Folktales 20

Biography 36

Myths 54

Technical Texts 74

Poetry 90

Informational Texts: *Social Studies* 106

Drama 128

Opinion Texts 146

Fairy Tales 162

Informational Texts: *Science* 178

Poetry 194

Informational Texts: *Science* 210

Realistic Fiction

What is realistic fiction?

Realistic fiction features characters and plots that could actually happen in everyday life. The settings are based on familiar places such as a home, school, office, or farm. The stories involve some type of conflict, or problem. The conflict can be something a character faces within himself, an issue between characters, or a problem between a character and nature.

What is the purpose of realistic fiction?

Realistic fiction shows how people grow and learn, deal with successes and failures, make decisions, build relationships, and solve problems. In addition to making readers think and wonder, realistic fiction is entertaining. Most of us enjoy "escaping" into someone else's life for a while.

How do you read realistic fiction?

Note the title, which will give you a clue about an important character or conflict in the story. As you read, pay attention to the thoughts, feelings, and actions of the main characters. Note how the characters change from the beginning of the story to the end. Ask yourself: *What moves this character to action? What is something I can learn from his or her struggles?*

The story takes place in an authentic setting.

At least one character deals with a conflict (self, others, or nature).

Features of
Realistic Fiction

The characters are like people you might meet in real life.

The story is told from a first person or third person point of view.

My Star Reader • Grade 4 • ©2016 Benchmark Education Company, LLC

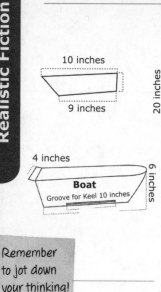

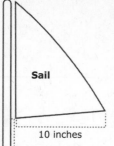

The Launch of the
Independence

Remember to jot down your thinking! →

1   Joe Evans and his dad were about to launch their small-scale sailboat. They had been building it in Dad's workshop all month. With the Fourth of July just a few days away, they had named their boat the *Independence*.

2   "Okay, let's get that sail on so we can get her into the water," Mr. Evans said.

3   While Joe and his dad secured the sail, Joe noticed some boys upstream watching their preparations. He could tell from the boys' expressions that they admired the boat.

4   Joe and his dad had spent many long hours constructing it. The assembly required sawing, carving, drilling, and sanding. They never took a shortcut during the entire production. They'd smoothed every rough edge and painted the boat with four coats. The inside was white, the outside and mast, blue, and the sail red and white. Yes, *Independence* made a perfect name for their creation.

5   As they set the boat into Little Sandy Stream, Mr. Evans whistled. "She's perfect, if I do say so myself. Now, there's just one thing left to do," he said, pulling out a long, thin cord. "We don't want to lose her on her maiden voyage."

6   He passed the cord to Joe, who <u>threaded</u> it through a hook on the boat and knotted it. Then they let the sailboat take off with the current. A light wind blew it gently along Little Sandy Stream. (Little Sandy Stream was a <u>misnomer</u> for this waterway: It wasn't "little," and it wasn't "sandy.")

7   As the sailboat drifted down the muddy stream, Joe and his dad followed along a path near the bank. From a distance, Joe thought it looked like a real vessel at sea. His dad was right: hard work did pay off.

Notes:

8   After a while, the stream widened and quickened. "Another half-mile and the Little Sandy runs into a river," his dad explained.

9   The sailboat passed by a family of ducks diving for food. The ducks flapped angrily as the *Independence* interrupted their lunch. Joe laughed at the indignant ducks, and then he tripped on a big root in the pathway.

10   "You okay, son?" his dad asked, helping Joe to his feet.

11   "I'm fine," Joe said, "but I dropped the cord." The line that had tethered the *Independence* to Joe was now loose in the stream. To make matters worse, the current was getting faster and faster as Little Sandy Stream neared the river. Joe and his dad raced along the path, trying frantically to keep their boat in sight. Unfortunately, they were losing the race. By now, only the red-and-white sail was visible from the path. Joe wondered what he'd do if he couldn't catch up with the *Independence.* He pushed that awful thought from his mind and pushed himself to run faster.

12   Just ahead of them, a thick forest was coming into view. "The Little Sandy picks up steam there, before running into the river," Joe's dad explained. "Our last hope is a mound that juts out right before the woods. If we can't grab our line there, we're going to lose the *Independence.*"

13   Some underbrush covering the pathway now blocked their view of the sailboat, but they kept pushing on. Somehow they made their way through the underbrush, and came out onto a sandy embankment—and a big surprise. The *Independence* was waiting there at the top of the mound like a marooned ship.

14   When they reached the boat, Joe found a napkin with a handwritten note on one side. It read, "This is a beautiful boat, and I'm sure you'll be looking for it. I'm happy that I was sitting here when it passed by. Have a happy Independence Day!"

Realistic Fiction

Find Text Evidence to Identify Theme

Theme	Text Evidence

My Star Reader • Grade 4 • ©2016 Benchmark Education Company, LLC

Find Text Evidence to Summarize the Text

Events

Summary

_____

_____

_____

_____

_____

_____

_____

_____

_____

_____

_____

_____

_____

_____

_____

_____

_____

_____

_____

_____

_____

_____

_____

_____

Text Evidence Questions

1. Describe how Joe feels about the *Independence.*

_____

Text Evidence:

_____

_____

2. In paragraph 5, Mr. Evans says, "We don't want to lose her on her maiden voyage." What does the phrase "maiden voyage" mean?

_____

Text Evidence:

_____

_____

_____

3. How can you tell that "The Launch of the *Independence*" is an example of realistic fiction?

_____

_____

Text Evidence:

_____

_____

4. Describe the point of view of the story's narrator.

_____

Text Evidence:

_____

_____

My Star Reader • Grade 4 • ©2016 Benchmark Education Company, LLC

Assessment Practice Questions

1. What is this story **mostly** about?

   A. father and son's day sailing their small sailboat

   B. the sailboat's trip down the river

   C. the Fourth of July

   D. the history of Little Sandy Stream

2. Which word is a synonym for <u>threaded</u> in paragraph 6?

   A. strung

   B. cleaned

   C. pulled

   D. tied

3. Reread paragraphs 6 and 7. Using examples from the paragraphs, explain what the word <u>misnomer</u> means. Why is Little Sandy Stream a misnomer?

   _____

   _____

   _____

   _____

A New World

1   *Home is like a dream*, Palma thought. She remembered her village on the Philippine island of Panay. That was home. She had lived near Tapaz. The palm trees grew wild there. The weather was either warm and muggy or rainy. People rode motorbikes to get around. Sometimes a whole family piled onto one bike. Shops and homes were open and inviting. No one wore long-sleeved shirts. The air smelled of cooking and flowers. People laughed and played together in the evenings.

2   Then Palma moved to Minneapolis, Minnesota. Everything was strange there. People lived all crammed together in a bustling, tall city. They rushed all the time, driving about in large cars. Ads flashed colorful pictures, music played, buses honked, and traffic lights changed over and over.

3   Palma and her grandmother had left Tapaz in October to live with her aunt and uncle, who had moved to Minneapolis many years before. The village had been at its hottest when they left. Insects buzzed, and people stayed indoors during the hot afternoons.

My Star Reader • Grade 4 • ©2016 Benchmark Education Company, LLC

Notes:

4   It was so different here! The weather was cold—colder than Palma had ever known. The air was like the inside of a refrigerator. Her breath was frosty in the mornings. She had to wear heavy coats and scarves, and still her nose and the tips of her ears got cold. Palma often stayed inside, where it was warm. She watched her favorite movie over and over again. It was about the Chinese heroine Mulan, whose father was getting old. Mulan pretended to be a boy so she could join the army in place of her father.

5   One afternoon the sky clouded over completely. It grew even colder. Palma pointed at the sky and asked Aunt May, "What's happening?"

6   Aunt May laughed. "You'll see, *mija*."

7   The clouds seemed to hang lower, and the sky grew darker. Inside, the heater ticked. Palma was grateful for its warmth. Just when Palma thought the sky would burst, white flakes began to fall.

8   "Auntie!" Palma cried in surprise.

9   Aunt May looked out the window. She smiled. "Ah, now it is time. Come along."

10   They bundled up in their warm clothes and went outside. The white flakes were drifting down faster and thicker. Palma had never seen anything like it! She held out her hand. A flake landed in the center of her palm. It was so small and light that she did not feel it until it melted.

11   "What is it called?" she asked.

12   "Snow," Aunt May answered. "It happens when rain gets very cold and freezes in the sky. Then it falls to Earth as soft, delicate flakes. Sometimes so many flakes fall that the snow piles up on the ground. It might even stay there all winter."

Notes:

13   They watched the snow for several minutes. People rushed about on the street as usual. No one else seemed to think the snow was strange. Palma made a little whining noise. Her eyes welled with tears.

14   "What is it, *mija?*" Auntie asked.

15   "I don't like it here. It's cold and strange, and now we have snow. I miss my friends and my village. I want to go home."

16   Auntie was quiet for a moment, thinking. Then she said, "I know that it is hard to move to a new place. It was hard for me, too. Remember the story of Mulan. She was brave for the good of her family. Your family lives here now. Can you be brave and courageous for us, too?"

17   Palma thought about it. "Yes," she decided finally, "I can do that."

18   She and Aunt May watched the snow for a bit longer. Then they went back inside. The snow was falling faster. Everything seemed quiet and peaceful. This new world was still strange to her, but she decided that it could be beautiful as well.

A New World

Notes:

Remember to annotate the text!

1   *Home is like a dream these days*, Palma thought. She remembered her village on the Philippine island of Panay with a dull ache. That was home. She had lived near Tapaz, where the palm trees grew wild and the weather was either muggy and warm or rainy. People rode motorbikes to get around, sometimes with a whole family piled aboard one bike. Shops and homes were open and inviting. No one wore long-sleeved shirts. The smell of cook smoke hung in the air, as did the fragrance of flowers. Friends and families laughed and played together in the evenings.

2   Then Palma moved to Minneapolis, Minnesota, where everything was strange. People lived all crammed together in a loud, bustling, tall city. They seemed to rush all the time, driving about in large cars. Ads flashed colorful pictures, music played, buses honked, and traffic lights changed over and over (red, green, yellow, red, green, yellow, in a never-ending cycle).

3   Palma and her grandmother had left Tapaz in October to live with her aunt and uncle, who had moved to Minneapolis many years before. The village had been at its hottest when they left. Insects buzzed all the time, and people stayed inside during the scorching afternoons.

Notes:

4   It was so different here! The weather was cold—colder than Palma had ever known. The air was like the inside of a refrigerator. Her breath was frosty in the mornings. She had to wear heavy coats and scarves, and still her nose and the tips of her ears got cold. Palma often stayed inside where it was warm, watching her favorite movie over and over again. It was about the Chinese heroine Mulan, whose father was getting old. Mulan pretended to be a boy so she could join the army in place of her father.

5   One afternoon the sky clouded over completely, and it grew even colder. Palma pointed at the sky and asked Aunt May, "What's happening?"

6   Aunt May laughed. "You'll see, *mija.*"

7   The clouds seemed to hang lower, and the sky grew darker as Palma watched from the window. The heater ticked on often. She was grateful for its warmth. Just when Palma thought the sky would burst, white flakes began to fall from above.

8   "Auntie!" Palma cried in surprise.

9   Aunt May came in from the kitchen and looked out the window. She smiled. "Ah, now it is time. Come along."

10   Together, they bundled up in their warm clothes and walked out of the apartment to the sidewalk. By now, the white flakes were drifting down faster and thicker. Palma had never seen anything like it! She held out her hand, and a flake landed in the center of her palm. It was so small and light that she did not feel it until it melted.

11   "What is it called?" she asked.

12   "Snow," Aunt May answered. "It happens when rain gets very cold and freezes in the sky. Then it falls to Earth as soft, delicate flakes. Sometimes so many flakes fall that the snow piles up on the ground, and it might stay there all winter."

13   They watched the snow for several quiet minutes. People rushed about on the street as usual. None of them seemed to think the snow was strange. Palma made a little whining noise. Her eyes welled with tears.

14   "What is it, *mija?*" Auntie asked.

15   "I don't like it here. It is cold and strange, and now we have snow. I miss my friends and my village. I want to go home."

16   Auntie was quiet for a moment, thinking. Then she said, "I know that it is hard to move to a new place. It was hard for me, too. Remember the story of Mulan, though. She was brave and courageous for the good of her family. Your family lives here now. Can you be brave and courageous for us, too?"

17   Palma thought about it. "Yes," she decided finally, "I can do that."

18   She and Aunt May stood and watched the snow for a bit longer before they went back inside. The snow was falling faster, and it made everything seem quiet and peaceful. This new world was still strange to her, but she decided that it could be beautiful as well.

Notes:

Text Evidence Questions

1. How is Palma's new home different from her old home?

_____

_____

Text Evidence:

_____

_____

_____

_____

2. What kind of sensory language is used in Paragraph 4 to help provide imagery for the reader?

_____

Text Evidence:

_____

3. Why does Aunt May compare Palma to the main character in the classic story of Mulan?

_____

_____

Text Evidence:

_____

_____

_____

4. How does Palma feel about her new home at the end of the story?

_____

Text Evidence:

_____

_____

Assessment Practice Questions

1. Part A

Which option **best** describes Palma's outlook at the beginning of the story?

    A. Palma loves the snow.

    B. Palma thinks that she should not live with Aunt May.

    C. Palma does not like the strangeness of Minnesota.

    D. Palma does not miss her home in Panay.

1. Part B

What event changes her outlook?

    A. Palma and Aunt May go for a walk in the snow.

    B. Aunt May tells her to think about the bravery of Mulan.

    C. Palma thinks about how sunny it is in Panay.

    D. Palma sits down to watch the movie *Mulan.*

2. How can a strange place be beautiful? Use examples from the passage to support your answer.

_____

_____

_____

_____

Realistic Fiction

Writing

When something is exciting, it is thrilling. You feel like you can't wait to see what happens next when you are excited. Use the chart to organize your writing. Then write a paragraph to give your opinion about "*The Launch of the* Independence." Remember to use words such as *for instance,* and *in order to,* to connect your opinion with reasons. Write your paragraph on the lines below.

Opinion:	
Reasons	**Text Evidence**

_____

_____

_____

_____

_____

Realistic Fiction

Vocabulary

1. Match each word from "The Launch of the *Independence*" with the correct prefix or suffix on the right.

preparations _____   **a.** suffix: "having qualities of"

unfortunately _____   **b.** prefix: "outside"

independence _____   **c.** prefix: "together"

frantically _____   **d.** prefix: "before"

expressions _____   **e.** prefix: "not"

constructing _____   **f.** suffix: "forming a noun"

2. Write a sentence that uses each of the words below.

preparations

_____

unfortunately

_____

independence

_____

frantically

_____

expressions

_____

constructing

_____

Folktales

What is a folktale?

A folktale is often a short story that is passed down from generations. Folktales are connected closely to legends. A folktale teaches a lesson, or moral. In folktales, it is common for the characters to have flaws. Characters can be animals.

What is the purpose of folktales?

Folktales often reflect the culture they came from. They can help explain the values of a certain culture. Folktales act as a way to record important themes. Folktales usually teach lessons about moral traits. Folktales can also explain why certain things happen in nature.

How do you read a folktale?

The title will often tell you who the main characters are, as well as the plot. Think about how the events of the story explain something in nature, or teach a lesson.

Who invented folktales?

While people have been telling folktales for many hundreds of years, it is hard to say exactly when the genre started.

My Star Reader • Grade 4 • ©2016 Benchmark Education Company, LLC

Features of a Folktale

The main characters can be animals.

The story is often short.

Characters often have a flaw or problem.

The story explains how something came to be in nature.

Characters learn a lesson.

Folktales

Remember to take notes! →

The Affair of the Hippopotamus and the Tortoise

1   Many years ago, the hippopotamus, whose name was Isantim, was one of the biggest kings on the land. He was second only to the elephant. The hippo had seven large, fat wives, of whom he was very fond. Now and then he used to give a big feast to the people. A curious thing was that, although everyone knew the hippo, no one, except his seven wives, knew his name.

2   At one of the feasts, just as the people were about to sit down, the hippo said, "You have come to feed at my table, but not one of you knows my name. If you cannot tell my name, you shall all go away without your dinner."

3   As they could not guess his name, they had to go away and leave all the good food behind them. But before they left, the tortoise stood up and asked the hippopotamus what he would do if he told him his name at the next feast. So the hippo replied that he would be so ashamed of himself that he and his whole family would leave the land. In the future they would dwell in the water.

MY STAR READER • GRADE 4 • ©2016 BENCHMARK EDUCATION COMPANY, LLC

4   Now it was the <u>custom</u> for the hippo and his seven wives to go down every morning and evening to the river to wash and have a drink. The tortoise was aware of this custom. The hippo used to walk first and the seven wives followed.

5   One day, when they had gone down to the river to bathe, the tortoise made a small hole in the middle of the path. . . . He half buried himself in the hole he had dug, leaving the greater part of his shell exposed. When the hippo's wives came along, the first one knocked her foot against the tortoise's shell. Immediately she called out to her husband, "Oh! Isantim, my husband, I have hurt my foot."

6   At this the tortoise was very glad. He went joyfully home, as he had found out the hippo's name.

7   When the hippo gave his next feast, he made the same condition about his name. The tortoise got up and said, "Do you promise you will not kill me if I tell you your name?" The hippo promised. The tortoise then shouted as loud as he was able, "Your name is Isantim!"

8   At that, a cheer went up from all the people, and then they sat down to their dinner.

9   When the feast was over, the hippo, with his seven wives, in accordance with his promise, went down to the river. They have lived in the water from that day till now. Although they come on shore to feed at night, you never find a hippo on land in the daytime.

Folktales

Find Text Evidence to Summarize the Text

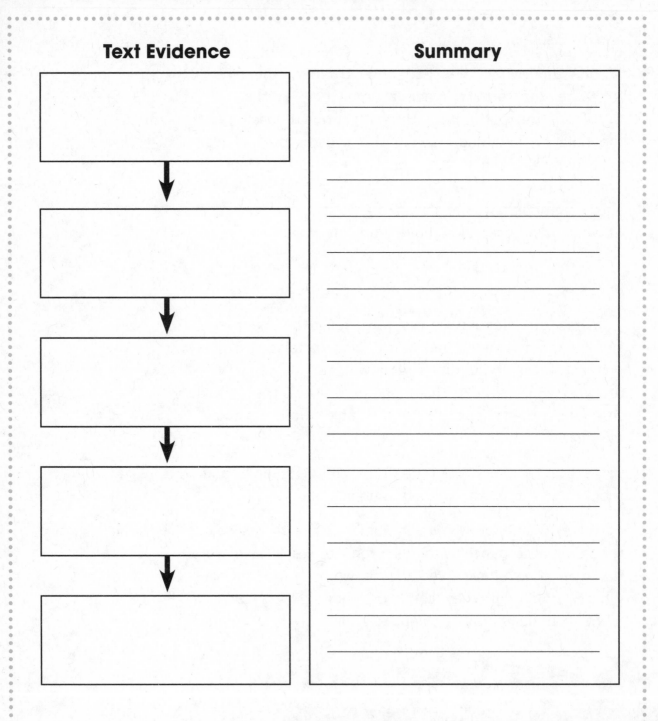

Text Evidence

Summary

Find Text Evidence to Identify Theme

Theme:	
Text Evidence:	

MY STAR READER • GRADE 4 • ©2016 BENCHMARK EDUCATION COMPANY, LLC

Text Evidence Questions

1. What is the message, or theme, of the story?

_____

Text Evidence:

_____

_____

_____

2. Which word in paragraph 9 has 3 syllables?

_____

Text Evidence:

_____

_____

3. Why does the tortoise bury himself partway into the ground?

_____

_____

Text Evidence:

_____

_____

4. What details from paragraph 9 let the reader know the story is a folktale?

_____

Text Evidence:

_____

_____

Assessment Practice Questions

1. What is the meaning of the word <u>custom</u> in paragraph 4?

   A. someone who buys goods

   B. clothes worn by a performer

   C. a tradition

   D. a law

2. Who is telling the story?

   A. Isantim

   B. a tortoise

   C. third person narrator

   D. unknown first person narrator

3. This folktale tells the tale of why hippopotami live in the water. What could be another theme of this folktale? Use examples from the passage to support your answer.

   _____

   _____

   _____

   _____

   _____

Kanchil and the Crocodiles

Remember to annotate the text as you read!

1   Kanchil, the little mouse deer, was hungry. A bush with juicy, ripe berries grew on the other side of the river.

2   *I do not have a boat. I cannot swim that far*, thought Kanchil. *How will I get to the other side of the river*?

3   Kanchil saw some crocodiles sleeping along the riverbank. He did not want to wake the crocodiles from their nap. Otherwise, he might become their snack!

4   *Unless . . .* , thought the clever mouse deer. He looked across the river at the bush with the juicy berries. Kanchil's mouth watered as a plan took shape. Kanchil picked up some pebbles. He tossed them softly toward Budi, the head crocodile.

5   "Hey!" called Budi, jumping up with a start. Getting woken up from a nap put Budi in a bad mood. Then again, Budi usually went to sleep in a bad mood, too. "What are you doing?" he grumbled.

6   "I am sorry to wake you, Budi. But I just came back from a visit with the king," said Kanchil.

7   "What does the king want with you? You better have a good answer, or I will eat you." The big crocodile showed Kanchil his big, sharp teeth.

Notes:

8   Budi and the crocodiles often threatened to eat Kanchil. But so far, they had not caught him. "The king asked me to count the crocodiles," Kanchil explained. "He wants to know how many crocodiles there are so he can give each of you a present."

9   Upon hearing the word *present*, the other crocodiles woke up. "Presents? I love presents," they said.

10   Budi had been tricked by Kanchil before. "Why does the king want to give us presents?" he asked.

11   "Well," said Kanchil. "I'm not supposed to tell. But if you promise not to tell that I told—"

12   "We promise! We promise!" said the eager crocodiles.

13   "The king wants to give the crocodiles a reward. You keep the river safe from . . . alligators . . . Now, line up so I can count you."

14   The crocodiles quickly lined up side by side, thinking about their presents. "No, no, no," said Kanchil. "I need you to line up end to end. That way, I won't leave anyone out."

15   The crocodiles then lined up end to end. They made a line that went across the river. "That's just right," Kanchil said. "Now I can count you. One, two, three . . ."

16   The little mouse deer counted crocodiles as he walked across them to the other side of the river. "Eight, nine, ten," he said, happily hopping off the head of Budi onto the riverbank. The berry bush was now within his reach.

17   "Thanks for letting me use you as a crocodile bridge," said the little mouse deer as he stuffed his face with berries.

18   "Kanchil tricked us again!" cried Budi. "I'll get you next time!"

19   "What about the presents?" asked the other crocodiles.

Folktales

Kanchil and the Crocodiles

Remember to jot down your thinking!

1   Kanchil, the little mouse deer, was hungry. Suddenly, he spied a bush with ripe, juicy berries that was growing on the other side of the river. His mouth watered at the sight, making him feel even hungrier.

2   *Alas, I don't own a boat, and I certainly can't swim that far*, thought Kanchil. *How will I ever get to the other side of the river to eat those berries?*

3   Kanchil noticed some crocodiles sleeping along the riverbank. He was afraid that if he roused the crocodiles from their nap they might decide to eat him for their snack. *Unless . . .* thought the clever mouse deer. He gazed across the river at the bush with its delicious berries, and gradually, a plan took shape in his mind. Kanchil picked up some pebbles, and he tossed them softly toward Budi, the head crocodile.

4   "Hey!" snarled Budi, awaking with a start. Whenever he was woken up from a nap, Budi's mood would quickly become foul. Of course, Budi's disposition wasn't all that pleasant to begin with. Usually he went to sleep in a bad mood, too. "What do you think you're doing?" Budi grumbled.

5   "I am sorry to wake you up from your slumber, Budi. However, I just returned from a visit with the king," explained Kanchil.

6   "What in the world would the king want with the likes of you?" he demanded. "You better have a good answer, or I will devour you whole!" The large crocodile grinned hungrily, making sure that Kanchil could get a glimpse of his sharp, gleaming teeth.

Notes:

7   Of course, Budi and the crocodiles routinely threatened to eat Kanchil. Fortunately for Kanchil, they had not been able to catch him yet. "The king asked me to take a census of all the crocodiles," Kanchil explained. "He wants to know exactly how many crocodiles there are so he can give each and every one of you a present."

8   Upon hearing the word *present*, the other crocodiles woke up. "Presents? I love presents," they all said.

9   Budi, however, was suspicious because he had been tricked by Kanchil before. "Why does the king want to give us presents?" he demanded.

10   "I'm not allowed to say, but I suppose that if you promise not to tell anyone that I told—" said Kanchil.

11   "We promise! We promise!" cried all the excited crocodiles.

12   "Okay, okay, but you must keep this information to yourselves," said Kanchil. "The king wants to give the crocodiles a reward because you keep the river safe from . . . alligators. . . . Now, line up so I can count you."

13   The crocodiles quickly lined up side by side, thinking eagerly about their presents. "No, no, no," said Kanchil. "I need you to line up end to end. That's the only way I can be sure I haven't left anyone out."

14   The crocodiles obediently lined up end to end, forming a line that went across the river. "That's perfect," Kanchil said. "Now I can count you all. One, two, three . . ."

15   As the little mouse deer counted crocodiles, he stepped across them to the other side of the river. "Eight, nine, ten," he said, happily hopping onto the riverbank.

16   "Thanks for letting me use you as a crocodile bridge," said the little mouse deer as he stuffed his face with berries.

17   "Kanchil tricked us again!" cried Budi. "I'll get you next time!"

18   "What about our presents?" asked the other crocodiles.

Independent
Workstation ★ **1**

Text Evidence Questions

1. What problem does Kanchil experience in the story?

_____

_____

Text Evidence:

_____

_____

2. Why do you think the story is called a "trickster tale"?

_____

_____

Text Evidence:

_____

_____

3. In paragraph 18, how do the words "Kanchil tricked us again!" go along with the illustration in the story and help the reader understand Kanchil's character?

_____

_____

Text Evidence:

_____

4. What point of view is the story's narrator? How can you tell?

_____

_____

Text Evidence:

_____

_____

My Star Reader • Grade 4 • ©2016 Benchmark Education Company, LLC

Assessment Practice Questions

1. **Part A**

   Which reason **best** explains why Kanchil has to trick the crocodiles so he is able to cross the river?

   A. Kanchil is afraid the crocodiles will eat him.

   B. The crocodiles are keeping the berries for themselves.

   C. The king asked Kanchil to trick the crocodiles.

   D. The crocodiles like practical jokes.

1. **Part B**

   Choose the sentence(s) from the passage that **best** supports your answer to part A.

   A. He did not want to wake the crocodiles from their nap. Otherwise, he might become their snack!

   B. "What does the king want with you? You better have a good answer, or I will eat you."

   C. The berry bush was now within his reach.

   D. The crocodiles quickly lined up side by side.

2. At what point do the crocodiles fall for Kanchil's trick? What does this say about the crocodiles?

   _____

   _____

   _____

   _____

Folktales

Writing

You learned that one of the features of a folktale is that it explains how something came to be in nature. Write about what the folktale "The Affair of the Hippopotamus and the Tortoise" tells about nature. Use the graphic organizer to identify text evidence to support your answer. Then write a paragraph to explain your answer on the lines below.

What the Story Explains About Nature	Text Evidence

_____

_____

_____

_____

_____

_____

_____

_____

Digging Deeper into Identifying Theme

1. The tortoise in "The Affair of the Hippopotamus and the Tortoise" is a trickster character. What are the traits of a trickster?

_____

_____

_____

2. What is the trickster trying to get by tricking other characters?

_____

_____

_____

3. What other stories have you read with trickster characters?

_____

_____

_____

Focus on the Genre

BIOGRAPHY

What is a biography?

A biography is a factual retelling of another person's life story. The person may have lived long ago or in recent history, or may still be alive today. Biographies can cover a person's entire life or just important parts. A biography often includes direct quotes from the person. This helps the reader make a connection to the person.

What is the purpose of a biography?

A biography helps a reader understand the important people, places, times, and events in the subject's life. It provides a summary of the person's life experiences and achievements. The way the author writes the biography helps a reader get a sense of the person as a real human being who had (and perhaps still has) an impact on the lives of others.

How do you read a biography?

The title will tell you the subject and may include something interesting about him or her. The first paragraph will try to "hook" the reader by capturing his or her attention. As you read, note the setting because it often influences what happens in a person's life. Pay close attention to the sequence of events in the person's life. Ask yourself: *Did this event happen to the person, or did the person make it happen? How did this event affect the person's life? What do I admire about this person?*

Who writes biographies?

People who write biographies want to learn more about others' life stories and how those people made their marks on the world. Some people write biographies because they are interested in a certain topic, such as sports, history, or cooking. Others write biographies because they are interested in people!

A biography tells the person's date and place of birth.

A biography tells about the person's family, childhood, and important events.

A biography starts with a strong "hook."

Features of a Biography

A biography describes the person's impact on the world.

A biography describes the person's personality and characteristics.

A biography quotes the person and/or people who knew the person.

Remember to highlight important information!

The Remarkable Life of Andrew Carnegie

1 Andrew Carnegie led a "rags-to-riches" life. Although he started out as a low-level factory worker, he became a captain of industry. After amassing a great fortune, he gave most of it away.

Early Years

2 Andrew Carnegie was born in Scotland in 1835. His father was a weaver. He had trouble finding work because steam-powered looms were taking over weavers' jobs. While the Carnegie family struggled, Andrew was learning lessons about being poor.

3 In 1848, the family left for America, hoping for a better life. Andrew's mother borrowed money to pay for the fare. The family settled in Pittsburgh, Pennsylvania. Soon, Andrew had a job in a textile factory, working as a bobbin boy at $1.20 per week.

The Path to Riches

4 Over the next ten years, Carnegie changed jobs and earned promotions. His hard work, determination, and intelligence impressed one supervisor after another. By 1859, he had worked his way up to Superintendent of the Pennsylvania Railroad, Western Division.

Notes:

5   As he made more money, Carnegie began putting it to work by investing in oil, bridges, railroads, telegraphs, and iron. By 1868, he was a wealthy thirty-three-year-old. At that point, he considered quitting business and devoting his time to helping others. Instead, he kept working and gaining even more wealth. Carnegie invested money in a new process for producing steel in his iron mills. Before long, Carnegie Steel was the greatest steel producer in the world.

Carnegie and His Workers

6   Carnegie came from a family that had fought for fairness for common workers. Over the years, he supported workers' rights, too.

7   Carnegie's business motto, however, was "watch costs and profits take care of themselves." Sometimes Carnegie put his interest in profits before his concern for his workers. In 1892, steelworkers at his plant went on strike. They refused to work until they got more pay. In response, Carnegie locked out the striking workers and hired armed guards. In the conflict, many strikers were killed. This clash with workers hurt Carnegie's reputation. People no longer thought of him as a friend of the worker.

Carnegie's Philanthropy

8   In 1901, Carnegie sold his steel company for $480 million, making him the richest man in the world. Even so, Carnegie believed, "The man who dies rich, dies disgraced." His next career was spent fulfilling this motto by giving away his wealth.

9   Carnegie believed that education was a key to life. No one in history did more to establish public libraries than he did. Using his own money, he set up more than 2,500 public libraries and supported many colleges and universities. At the time of his death in 1919, he had succeeded in living up to his motto and had given away most of his fortune.

Biography

Find Text Evidence to Make Inferences

What I Read	What I Know	My Inference

MY STAR READER • GRADE 4 • ©2016 BENCHMARK EDUCATION COMPANY, LLC

Find Text Evidence to Summarize the Text

Events

Summary

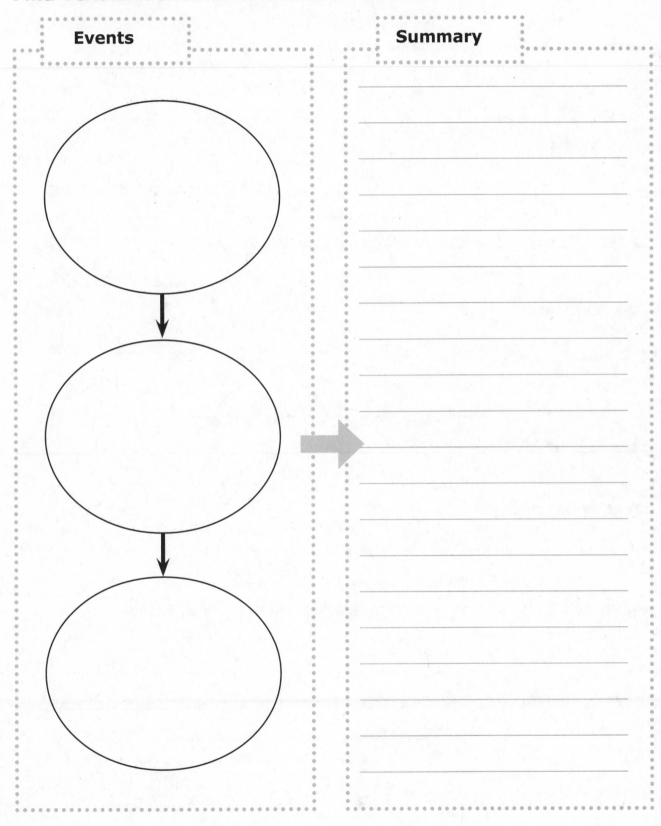

Text Evidence Questions

1. Which detail in the passage suggests that Andrew Carnegie wanted to spread his appreciation for education?

_____

_____

Text Evidence:

_____

_____

2. What is the section "The Path to Riches" mainly about?

_____

Text Evidence:

_____

_____

_____

3. The purpose of this selection is —

_____

Text Evidence:

_____

_____

4. A description of Carnegie's motto is included with the selection most likely to —

_____

Text Evidence:

_____

_____

_____

Assessment Practice Questions

1. Part A

What do you think **most likely** influenced Andrew Carnegie's beliefs about money?

A. the steelworker's strike in 1892

B. selling his steel company for $480 million

C. moving to Pennsylvania from Scotland

D. his family's hardships when he was young

1. Part B

Which context clue from the passage **best** supports your answer to part A?

A. "In 1848, the family left for America, hoping for a better life."

B. "Even so, Carnegie believed, 'The man who dies rich, dies disgraced.'"

C. "While the Carnegie family struggled, Andrew was learning lessons about being poor."

D. "By 1868, he was a wealthy thirty-three-year-old."

_____

2. What happened to Carnegie in 1892? Why do you think this is an important event?

_____

_____

_____

_____

_____

Biography

George Washington

Remember to take notes! →

Life in Virginia

1   George Washington was born on a large farm in Virginia on February 22, 1732. As a boy, George loved the open fields and mysterious forests. He liked to hunt, and to ride horses. He liked to farm the fertile land of his home. When he was a young man, George became a surveyor. He measured land and made maps. He went deep into the wilderness of Virginia. He camped and learned to take care of himself in dangerous situations. When George was just twenty-one years old, he became a soldier. He fought with the British against the French.

2   George proved himself to be a strong leader. He earned a promotion to <u>colonel</u>. In 1759, George married. He and his wife, Martha, settled down to a quiet life. They lived on a spacious farm called Mount Vernon. He filled his days by running the farm, hunting, fishing, and helping to raise Martha's two children. But these happy and peaceful times did not last. George Washington took part in the decision to declare independence.

Revolution!

3   By 1775, there were thirteen colonies. The people who lived in the colonies followed laws made by the British king, George III. They paid taxes to Britain. The colonists wanted to choose their own leaders and make their own laws. They wanted to make their

Notes:

own decisions about taxes. They wanted their own government.

4   Leaders from the colonies met in Philadelphia to talk about what to do. These leaders made an important decision: they would separate from Britain. They would fight for freedom if they had to. In April 1775, the colonies went to war with Britain. To fight, they had to form an army. They chose George Washington to lead it. He was forty-three years old.

Leader in War

5   Washington had been a hero in the French and Indian War twenty years earlier. Now he would fight against the British as General George Washington. Few generals ever faced a greater challenge. The British had the strongest army and the biggest navy in the world. How could thirteen small colonies defeat them? The revolution was long and bloody. Most of Washington's soldiers had little training. Washington sometimes had no money to pay them. Supplies were short. It was often hard to get food.

6   How did a small, poorly trained army fight the awesome military power of Britain? They had Washington as their leader! To build a better army, Washington used the skills he developed in the wilderness of Virginia. He taught his men to travel light and to move quickly and quietly. He showed them how to hide in the woods. He made surprise attacks on the enemy.

7   Washington's men loved him and would do anything for him. He did not let them give up and he did not give up himself. He begged for supplies for his men. He once wrote that the men had "not even the shadow of a blanket" to keep warm in the bitter cold. The British had a large army, but the United States had George Washington. Washington's army faced great hardship at Valley Forge, Pennsylvania, during one cold winter of the Revolution.

Notes:

8   At first, Washington's army suffered many defeats. Holding his men together was difficult. During the terrible winter of 1777, Washington and his soldiers camped in the icy snow at Valley Forge, Pennsylvania. Many soldiers had no shoes or warm clothing. They were hungry. Even Washington grew discouraged. "I am wearied almost to death," he wrote. Many of his soldiers were ready to give up and leave for home. But Washington and his soldiers stayed to fight on. In 1781, after six years of fighting, the colonies won their freedom. The United States of America was born.

9   A new leader for a new country, Washington said that the only reward he wanted for his hard work was the "affection of a free people." He returned to a quiet life at Mount Vernon. He expected to spend the rest of his days there. But again his peaceful farming life did not last. His country was forging a new nation. The country needed a leader with courage and strength. The people wanted someone with common sense and experience. Washington was the ideal choice.

10   The United States was a new country with a new set of laws. The people had a new way of governing. Instead of having a king, they would vote for a leader. Washington was the one man everyone trusted to get the new government started. "Liberty, when it begins to take root, is a plant of rapid growth," he wrote to James Madison in March 1788. Washington won the election and became president of the new nation.

George Washington

Remember to annotate the text!

Life in Virginia

1   George Washington was born on a large farm in Virginia on February 22, 1732. As a boy, George loved the open fields and mysterious forests. He liked to hunt, ride horses, and farm the fertile land of his home. When he was a young man, George became a surveyor. He measured land and made maps, traveling deep into the wilderness of Virginia. He also learned how to survive in dangerous situations. When George was just twenty-one years old, he became a soldier and fought with the British against the French.

2   George proved himself to be a leader and was promoted to colonel. In 1759, George married and moved with his wife, Martha, to a spacious farm called Mount Vernon. He filled his days running the farm, hunting, fishing, and helping to raise Martha's two children. His happy and peaceful days came to an end when George decided to take part in the fight for independence.

Notes:

_____

_____

_____

_____

_____

_____

_____

_____

_____

_____

_____

_____

_____

_____

_____

_____

_____

_____

_____

_____

_____

_____

_____

_____

_____

Revolution!

3   By 1775, there were thirteen colonies. The people who lived in the colonies followed laws made by the British king, George III, and they paid taxes to Britain. The colonists wanted to choose their own leaders and make their own laws. Most of all, they wanted to make their own decisions about taxes.

4   Leaders from the colonies met in Philadelphia to discuss what actions to take. Together, these leaders reached an important decision. They would break away from Britain even if that meant fighting for freedom. In fact, in April 1775, the colonies went to war with Britain. In order to wage a war, they first had to form an army. They chose George Washington to lead the army. He was forty-three years old.

Leader in War

5   Twenty years earlier, Washington had served with the British in the French and Indian War. Now he would be General George Washington, fighting against them. Few generals in history have ever faced a tougher challenge. At the time, Britain had the strongest army and the biggest navy in the world.

6   What chance did thirteen small colonies have to defeat such a powerful foe? The revolution was long and bloody, and many of Washington's soldiers had no training. Sometimes Washington had no money to pay his soldiers, and little food or supplies to give them. How did a small, poorly trained army fight the awesome military power of Britain? Fortunately, they had Washington as their leader! To forge a stronger army, Washington used all the skills he had learned in the wilderness of Virginia. He taught his men to travel light and to move quickly and quietly. He showed them how to hide in the woods and then launch surprise attacks.

7   Washington's men were devoted to him and would do anything for him. He did not let them give up and he did not give up himself. He begged for supplies for his men. Once he wrote that the men had "not even the shadow of a blanket" to keep warm in the bitter cold. The British had a large army, but the United States had George Washington. Washington's army faced great hardship at Valley Forge, Pennsylvania, during one cold winter of the Revolution.

8   At first, Washington's army suffered many defeats. Simply holding his men together was difficult. During the terrible winter of 1777, Washington and his soldiers camped in the icy snow at Valley Forge. Many soldiers had no shoes or warm clothing, and they were hungry and tired. Even Washington grew discouraged. "I am wearied almost to death," he wrote. Many of his soldiers were ready to give up and go home, but Washington and his soldiers stayed to fight on.

9   In 1781, after six years of fighting, the colonies won their freedom, and the United States of America was born. Washington said that the only reward he wanted was the "affection of a free people." He returned to Mount Vernon, where he hoped to spend the rest of his days. But once again, his peaceful farming life did not last. His country was forging a new nation and needed a leader with courage and strength. The people wanted someone with common sense and experience, and Washington was the ideal choice.

10   The United States was a new country with a new kind of government. Instead of having a king, they would vote for a leader. Washington was the one man that everyone trusted to lead the new government. "Liberty, when it begins to take root, is a plant of rapid growth," he wrote to James Madison in March 1788. Washington won the election and became president of the new nation.

Notes:

Independent
Workstation **1**

Text Evidence Questions

1. What is the genre of the selection, and how can you tell?

_____

_____

Text Evidence:

_____

_____

2. What is the section "Leader in War" mainly about?

_____

_____

Text Evidence:

_____

_____

_____

3. What were the challenges of the soldiers fighting at Valley Forge?

_____

Text Evidence:

_____

_____

4. Why did the new nation vote for Washington as their first leader?

_____

Text Evidence:

_____

_____

Assessment Practice Questions

1. Using context clues, what is the **best** definition of the word <u>colonel</u> found in paragraph 2?

   A. a piece of corn

   B. an early settlement

   C. a ranking of a military officer

   D. a farmer

2. Why was George Washington chosen to be the first president of the United States? Choose all that apply.

   A. He fought a lot of battles in the American Revolution.

   B. He sided with the British to fight the French.

   C. People trusted him.

   D. He had common sense and experience.

3. How did George Washington contribute to the American Revolution?

   _____

   _____

   _____

   _____

Biography

Writing

In 1901, Andrew Carnegie was the world's richest person.
Why do you think he believed "the man who dies rich, dies disgraced"?

Use examples from the selection when writing your response.
Use the inference chart to help you organize your ideas. Then write your response on the lines below.

Text Clues	Inference

_____

_____

_____

_____

_____

My Star Reader • Grade 4 • ©2016 Benchmark Education Company, LLC

Vocabulary

1. Review the following words from "The Remarkable Life of Andrew Carnegie." Sort the words in the box into the correct categories below.

factory	fortune	industry
investing	profits	promotions
superintendent	supervisor	wealth

Business World	Money

2. Use words from each category to explain how money and the business world are related.

_____

_____

_____

_____

_____

MYTHS

What is a myth?

A myth is a story that explains something that occurs in nature. It might tell how the world began or explain why the world is the way it is. Usually the main character in a myth is a god or goddess or a hero with special powers. Sometimes the hero in a myth is on a quest, a journey in search of adventure.

What is the purpose of a myth?

Long ago, people believed myths to be true. They relied on these stories to explain events they did not understand, like violent storms or why there is night and day. Today, myths help us see what events confused or interested people long ago. The explanations in myths are creative and fun. They are exciting, too.

How do you read a myth?

The title of a myth often tells what event in nature the myth explains. Think about how the event is explained when you read a myth. Look for a hero with extraordinary powers. Ask yourself: *What does this hero do? How do the hero's actions help explain an event?*

Who invented myths?

In ancient times, storytellers told myths to answer questions about the world. Their listeners understood the heroes of these myths. They were heroes with human qualities similar to their own, but their superpowers meant that they could perform amazing deeds. In an ancient Greek myth, a god gives humans the gift of fire. In another myth, a Greek goddess explains the change of seasons. A Mexican god takes a dangerous journey to his homeland in a different myth. As the centuries passed, these stories were told and retold and then written down. Today, readers still enjoy the exciting adventures of these heroes.

My Star Reader • Grade 4 • ©2016 Benchmark Education Company, LLC

FEATURES OF A MYTH

Myths have characters that are humans, or human-like, and experience human emotions.

Myths often take place before time, or recorded history as we know it, began.

Myths often explain the origins of the world and its creatures.

Myths have gods, goddesses, heroes, and fantastic creatures with supernatural powers.

Characters often perform heroic tasks or go on quests.

Myths often explain the worldview of a people or culture and may have religious elements.

Myths

The Girl Who Saved the Village

Remember to highlight important information!

1   Long, long ago, there stood a small and humble village in the valley of a great mountain. The people of the village had no riches, but they had golden fields of wheat and emerald hills of grass for their sheep, so they were happy.

2   But one day, when the Sun Goddess Sola chose the top of their mountain as her new home, the rain stopped falling. A drought descended upon the village like a nightmare from which no one could awaken. Without wheat to bake bread, the villagers became weak. Without lush grass to eat, the sheep became sickly. The people were becoming desperate. But just as it is sometimes <u>darkest before the dawn</u>, a baby girl named Sage was born.

Notes:

3   From the moment of her birth, it was clear that Sage was unique. "She seems to radiate with pure delight, just like the sun!" her father would brag, and it was true. As she grew up, villagers would go out of their way just to stand near Sage. They loved to feel her powerful joy warm their hearts like the rays of the sun.

4   Sadly, Sage's parents' love for their daughter turned into a poisonous pride. As she grew older, they began to believe that their daughter was superior. "She will achieve what no one else can, you'll see," her father boasted. He became obsessed with the glory Sage would surely bring. So no one was surprised when he declared that Sage was going up the mountain to confront Sola.

5   "Order Sola to leave, Sage," her mother swooned, "and we will be royalty in this dusty little village!"

Notes:

6   With a heavy heart, Sage set out for the mountain. She climbed until she came to a garden filled with strange flowers that seemed to flicker like flames. A tiny woman sat at the edge of a small pond. She was watching tiny, ruby red fish swim in circles. "Hello, traveler," said the woman. "What brings you to this place above the clouds?"

7   Sage sighed. "I have come to ask the Sun Goddess to leave. My village has been suffering from a drought for a long time, and if she does not move from this mountain, everything and everyone will die."

8   "Oh, I'm sure Sola was not aware of your suffering!" said the woman. "You've asked so politely that Sola surely will agree to visit the other mountains of the world. But why are you still troubled?"

9   "I'm glad the drought will end, but my success brings another kind of trouble. My parents will expect to live as royalty now. Their pride has made them forget who they are."

10   The tiny woman then stood. It was Sola herself! A blazing white light surrounded her. The garden air seemed to shimmer. With a kind but sad voice she spoke. "Sage, I will leave this mountain and the rains will fall. But a new drought will begin—a drought of the heart. Your parents will gain glory, but they will lose what is truly important—humility, love, and you. You will be like a stranger to them. Only when they become aware of their folly and change their foolish ways will they recognize you as their beloved daughter once again. May it not take them long."

11   With those words, Sola rose and streaked across the sky like a kite of blinding white fire. Almost immediately, the rain began to fall, and Sage started trudging toward home. The valley would soon turn green and there would be plenty of food for all. But for the first time in her life, Sage could not smile.

Find Text Evidence to Identify the Voice of the Narrator

Title	Point of View	Text Evidence

Find Text Evidence to Identify Theme

Theme	
Text Evidence	

My Star Reader • Grade 4 • ©2016 Benchmark Education Company, LLC

Text Evidence Questions

1. In paragraph 10, how does the author use sensory language and imagery to describe what Sola thinks will happen to Sage?

_____

_____

Text Evidence:

_____

_____

2. If the story were written from the first person point of view from Sage's viewpoint, how would paragraph 5 be written?

_____

Text Evidence:

_____

_____

3. Identify the theme of the story and use evidence to explain your answer.

_____

_____

Text Evidence:

_____

_____

4. How can you describe the relationship between Sage and Sola once they meet each other?

_____

Text Evidence:

_____

_____

_____

Assessment Practice Questions

1. Part A

What does <u>darkest before the dawn</u> in paragraph 2 mean?

A. Things get worse before they get better.

B. The sun will not rise at night.

C. It's dark out before babies are born.

D. Bad things must happen for there to be good.

1. Part B

What sentences or phrases from the second paragraph **best** support your answer to part A? Choose all that apply.

A. The people were becoming desperate.

B. . . . a baby girl named Sage was born.

C. A drought descended upon the village like a nightmare.

D. All of the above.

_____

2. Explain why Sage is unhappy about the drought ending. Use examples from the passage to support your answer.

_____

_____

_____

_____

_____

Medusa
A Greek Myth

Remember to take notes! →

1   Long ago, there lived a beautiful young woman named Medusa. She had long, curly hair that shone like a mirror in the sunlight. Every young man wanted her as his wife.

2   But there was a problem. Medusa was vain. She liked to look at herself in the mirror. She loved to brag about her beauty. She bragged and bragged and bragged.

3   Medusa made the other women feel plain and ugly. They felt hurt and upset. They disliked her for her bragging even more than for her beauty. Whenever they saw Medusa in town, they would walk the other way. This sometimes meant doing silly things to distract their husbands.

4   But Medusa craved attention. As soon as someone looked at her, she would start her bragging.

5   "Look at my shiny, curly hair," Medusa said to the miller's wife.

6   "My cheeks are like two roses," she said to the baker's wife.

7   "Have you ever seen anyone as perfect and lovely as me?" she asked the butcher's wife.

Notes:

8   Most of the women learned to ignore Medusa; yet, the goddess Athena could not.

9   Athena was the goddess of wisdom. She was also the protector of art. That meant it was her duty to protect art and wise creations. One day, Medusa was visiting the holy temple of Athena. The temple was filled with beautiful sculptures, paintings, and colored glass. It was a place for worship.

10   But Medusa <u>mocked</u>, or made fun of, the art in the temple.

11   "Those sculptures are plain and boring," said Medusa.

12   "Those paintings look as if infants made them," she added.

13   "I could paint better than that!" she boasted.

14   That was a mistake. But then Medusa made a HUGE mistake. She pointed to a painting of Athena. "Think how much more beautiful that painting would be if I were the subject!" she sniffed with her nose in the air.

15   Athena heard Medusa. Athena's anger boiled and steamed. But being the goddess of wisdom, she decided to calm down.

16   The next day, Medusa was sitting by the river, gazing at her reflection. Along came the god Poseidon. Poseidon was the god of the rivers and the sea. Poseidon took one look at Medusa and could hardly breathe. He sat beside her just to talk. He felt more handsome just by talking to this beautiful woman. Medusa loved his attention.

17   Athena saw Medusa, a human, talking to Poseidon, a god. She became angry again. "How dare that vain, selfish human try to get a god for a husband," Athena said to herself. "He is supposed to like ME!"

Notes:

18   Once Poseidon left, she approached Medusa. "You foolish, foolish mortal! You dare to disgrace my temple. You dare to talk to a god as a boyfriend. You are not worthy!" Athena screamed.

19   "That's silly," said Medusa. "I can't help being beautiful. I can't help being perfect in every way. People feel happy when they look at me."

20   "Ugh!" Athena growled. "Beauty fades. But kindness and honesty are forever!" And with that, Athena used her powers to turn Medusa's shiny, curly hair into a snarl of slithering snakes.

21   "This is your punishment for being too vain," Athena exclaimed. "If you ever look at your reflection again, beware. You will turn to stone as soon as you see your face!"

22   And with that, Medusa was sent to the ends of Earth. She lived with monsters in a dark, muddy place.

23   What happened to Medusa is a lesson to others: control your pride!

Medusa
A Greek Myth

Notes:

Remember to annotate the text as you read! ←

1   Long ago, there lived a beautiful young woman named Medusa. She had long, curly hair that shone like a mirror in the sunlight. Every young man in the kingdom wanted her as his wife.

2   But there was a problem. Medusa was exceptionally vain, and she loved to gaze at her own reflection in the mirror. And if she wasn't looking at herself, she was bragging about her breathtaking beauty. All day long, she bragged and bragged and bragged.

3   Medusa not only made the other women feel plain and ugly, she trampled on their feelings and upset them. In fact, they hated her more for her incessant bragging than for being so beautiful. Whenever they spotted Medusa in town, they would dash off in another direction. At times, this also meant the women would do silly things to distract their husbands from noticing Medusa.

4   But still, Medusa could never get enough attention. As soon as someone glanced at her, Medusa would start bragging and boasting.

5   "Take a look at my gorgeous hair," Medusa said to the miller's wife.

6   "Don't you agree that my cheeks look like two roses?" she asked the baker's wife.

Myths

Notes:

7   "Have you ever seen anyone as perfect and lovely as me?" she asked the butcher's wife.

8   Most of the women learned to ignore Medusa. However, Athena, who was the goddess of wisdom, simply could not ignore Medusa.

9   One day, Medusa was visiting the temple of Athena. Since Athena was also the protector of art, her temple was filled with beautiful sculptures, paintings, and colored glass.

10   The holy temple was a place for worship, but that didn't stop Medusa from mocking the art. "Those sculptures are plain and boring," said Medusa. "Those paintings look as if they were made by infants! I could paint better than that!" she boasted.

11   And then Medusa committed an even more outrageous, unforgivable crime. She pointed to a painting of Athena. "Think how much more beautiful that painting would be if I were the subject instead!" She sniffed with her nose in the air.

12   Athena heard Medusa's arrogant words, and her anger boiled and steamed. But being the goddess of wisdom, Athena decided to calm down before she took action.

13   The next day, Medusa was sitting by the river, and as usual she was gazing adoringly at her own reflection. Along came Poseidon, the god of the rivers and the sea. Poseidon took one look at Medusa and was so smitten that he could hardly breathe. He sat beside her and began to talk, feeling more handsome just by being near such a beautiful woman. Medusa was delighted to be the object of the god's attention.

14   When Athena saw Medusa, a human, talking to Poseidon, a god, she became enraged. "How dare that vain, selfish human try to get a god for a husband!" Athena said to herself. "He is supposed to like ME!"

Notes:

15   Once Poseidon left, Athena approached Medusa. "You foolish, foolish mortal! You dare to disgrace my temple. You dare to talk to a god as a boyfriend. You are not worthy!" Athena screamed.

16   "That's silly," said Medusa. "I can't help being beautiful. I can't help being perfect in every way. People feel happy when they look at me."

17   "Ugh!" Athena growled. "Beauty fades, but kindness and honesty are forever!" And with that, Athena used her powers to turn Medusa's shiny, curly hair into a snarl of slithering snakes.

18   "This is your punishment for being too vain," Athena exclaimed. "If you ever look at your reflection again, you will turn to stone as soon as you see your face! Beware!"

19   And with that, Medusa was sent to the ends of Earth. She lived with monsters in a dark, muddy place.

20   What happened to Medusa is a lesson to others: control your pride!

Text Evidence Questions

1. What is a good summary of the story?

_____

_____

_____

Text Evidence:

_____

_____

_____

_____

2. Why does Athena think she is better than Medusa?

_____

Text Evidence:

_____

_____

_____

_____

3. What does Medusa think of the art she sees in Athena's temple?

_____

Text Evidence:

_____

_____

_____

4. Which phrase in paragraph 10 helps the reader understand the meaning of the word <u>mocked</u>?

_____

MY STAR READER • GRADE 4 • ©2016 BENCHMARK EDUCATION COMPANY, LLC

Assessment Practice Questions

1. What line **best** reflects the theme of this myth?

   A. "Beauty fades. But kindness and honesty are forever!"

   B. "What happened to Medusa is a lesson to others: control your pride!"

   C. "But being the goddess of wisdom, she decided to calm down."

   D. "Most of the women learned to ignore Medusa; yet, the goddess Athena could not."

2. Which option **mostly** describes how the narrator's voice shapes Medusa's personality?

   A. The narrator makes Medusa out to be ugly.

   B. The narrator makes Medusa out to be beautiful and perfect.

   C. The narrator leads the reader to believe that Medusa is humble.

   D. The narrator makes Medusa out to be beautiful, but far from perfect.

3. What are the key events that lead up to Medusa's transformation?

   _____

   _____

   _____

   _____

   _____

Writing

The character of Sage in "The Girl Who Saved the Village" changes from the beginning of the passage to the end of the passage.

Write about how Sage feels at the beginning of the passage and how her feelings change by the end of the passage. Use the graphic organizer to identify text evidence from each story to support your answer. Then write a paragraph to explain your answer on the lines below.

	Sage's Feelings
Beginning	
End	

_____

_____

_____

_____

_____

Read Across the Texts

1. Compare "The Remarkable Life of Andrew Carnegie" on page 38 with "The Girl Who Saved the Village" on page 56. How are the texts alike? How are they different?

_____

_____

_____

_____

Text Evidence:

_____

_____

_____

_____

_____

_____

_____

2. Fill in the Venn diagram. Write details about "Andrew Carnegie" on the left. Compare it to "The Girl Who Saved the Village" on the right. Write details that are the same about both people in the midddle section.

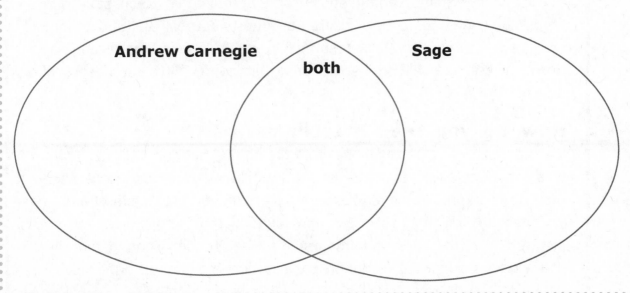

Andrew Carnegie   **Sage**

both

Technical Texts

What is a technical text?

A technical text is written direction that tells how to make or do something. We use technical texts every day! We make soup using a recipe in a cookbook. We learn new math skills by following the steps in a textbook. We learn to play new board games by reading the rules that come in the box. Adults use technical texts at home, in their jobs, and in their hobbies. Other names for technical texts are technical writing, instructions, directions, or how-tos.

What is the purpose of a technical text?

A technical text describes how to do something in a way other people can understand. The author clearly explains what supplies and equipment to use and what steps to follow. Some authors share tips they've learned from personal experience that will help the process go more smoothly for readers. They often include one or more photographs, illustrations, or diagrams to help readers visualize, or see, how to do the steps. Sometimes they include a picture of the finished product as well.

Who is the audience for a technical text?

People of all ages use technical texts to learn new skills, perform science experiments, administer first aid, build, cook or bake foods, play games, create crafts, or improve their abilities in music or sports. People can find technical texts in books, magazines, newspapers, pamphlets, instructions that come with purchases, and on the Internet.

How do you read a technical text?

You can choose a technical text by its title. The title will tell you what you can learn to make or do by reading the text. Next check the list of supplies and equipment to see if you have everything you need. After that, read through all the steps and study the pictures to make sure you understand what to do. Then begin! As you work, pay special attention to any tips the author provides.

Features of a Technical Text

The title clearly identifies the topic.

The author includes photographs, illustrations, or diagrams.

The introduction tells why the reader will want to make or do the activity or project.

Most sentences begin with verbs. The sentences are short and direct.

Supplies and equipment are listed in the order in which they are used.

The directions are given as numbered steps or short paragraphs with sequence words.

How to Build a Japanese Fighter Kite

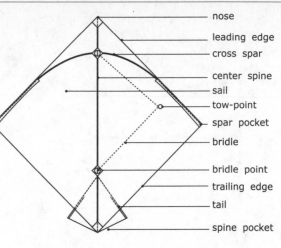

nose
leading edge
cross spar
center spine
sail
tow-point
spar pocket
bridle
bridle point
trailing edge
tail
spine pocket

Remember to jot down your thinking!

1   The people of Japan have been building fighter kites for hundreds of years. Now you, too, can build a Japanese kite.

2   Fighter kites are maneuverable, single-line kites, very much like the kind you may have flown yourself. Most kites use a long tail to keep stable. Fighting kites, on the other hand, are all about movement and maneuverability. They are designed to respond sharply to each tug on the line.

3   As you practice controlling a fighter kite, you'll discover how the kite becomes a living thing. The more practice you get, the clearer it will be that tugs on the line are a language all their own. Mastering a fighter kite takes constant focus and deft fingers. After much practice, you may discover skills you never knew you had. Some people find kite flying very restful too because focusing on the kite helps clear your mind of other thoughts or worries.

Kite Components

4   Today, most fighting kites are basically square or diamond shaped. Historically, though, they came in every shape and size. No matter what the shape, the basic scientific principles of flight influence the design.

5   What are the key features of a fighter kite? The kite's basic fabric is called the *sail*. The sail can be made of anything from newspaper to nylon to high-tech plastic. The material simply needs to be light and strong with a smooth surface.

6   To stretch the sail you need a frame. The backbone of this frame is a rigid stick called the *spine*. The spine stiffens the kite from top to bottom.

7   The next part of the fighter's frame is a horizontal stick called the *cross spar.* The spar spreads the sail from side to side. Spars can be made of wood, bamboo, fiberglass, or even carbon fiber. The ends of the spar fit into fabric pockets to attach to the sail. These pockets help bend the spar, giving it a bow-like shape that keeps the sail stiff and flat. The bend improves stability.

8   The lines that attach to the kite are called bridle lines. There might be two or three of these. They attach to the single flying line at what is called the *tow-point.* The placement of the bridle points, or connections, creates the angle at which the kite faces the wind. The bridle lines also spread the wind's force across the kite's frame, giving it more stability.

9   Fighters can have other features, such as holes in the sail, tails, or stiffening sticks called *battens.* Kites may be decorated with bright colors or symbols too, or they may be plain. But the model described here has all the basic features you'll need in your first fighter kite.

Find Text Evidence to Identify Sequence of Events

Step 1	Text Evidence:
Step 2	**Text Evidence:**
Step 3	**Text Evidence:**

Find Text Evidence to Summarize the Text

Key Details

Summary

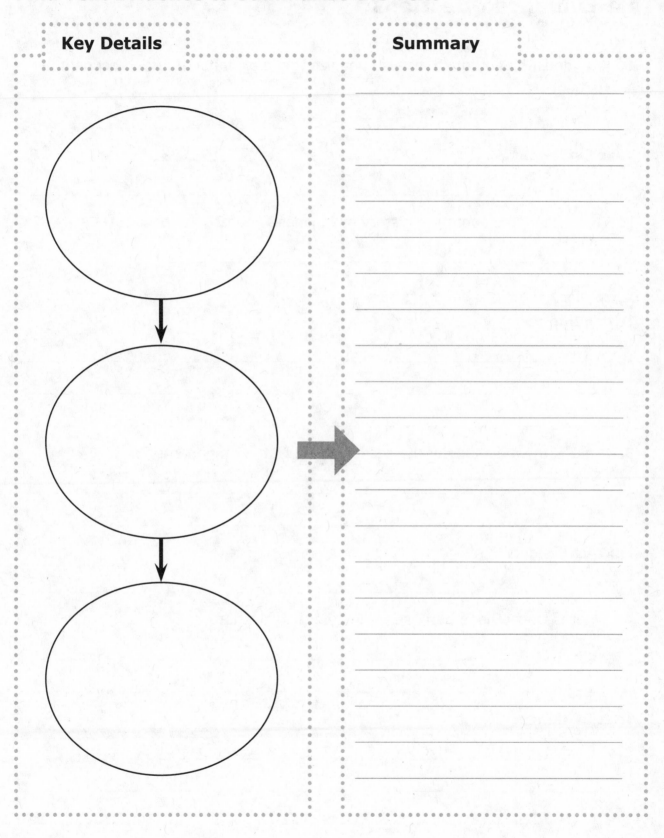

Text Evidence Questions

1. Why does the author choose to organize the information in the selection in a sequence?

_____

Text Evidence:

_____

2. The author tells about the history of Japanese fighter kites because —

_____

_____

Text Evidence:

_____

_____

_____

3. What is the main idea of the section called "Kite Components"?

_____

_____

Text Evidence:

_____

4. What is the author's purpose for writing the selection?

_____

_____

Text Evidence:

_____

_____

_____

MY STAR READER • GRADE 4 • ©2016 BENCHMARK EDUCATION COMPANY, LLC

Assessment Practice Questions

1. What is **most likely** the reason why the diagram is included at the top of this passage?

    A. to show the reader how pretty the kites can be

    B. to illustrate the key features of the kite

    C. to give directions on how to assemble the kite

    D. to show how the line tugs on the kite

2. Look at the boxes below. Select the option that **best** completes the diagram.

Choose sail material.	→	?	→	Add cross spar.

    A. Stretch sail over the frame.

    B. Attach bridle lines.

    C. Build frame for kite.

    D. Add battens to the kite.

3. Do you think you could build a kite following the directions and using the diagram in this passage? If not, what would help you build it?

    _____

    _____

    _____

    _____

Sun Charts

Full Sun   Partial Sun   Shade

The Secret to Great Gardens

1   Warm sunshine feels good! Sunlight gives your body vitamin D, so it is good for you too. Still, too much sunlight can cause burns and even serious illness. It's important for people to get some sun, just not too much.

2   The same is true for plants. Plants are healthiest with just the right amount of sunlight. That's the biggest secret to having a great garden.

3   Would you like to plant a garden? Maybe you have a little space in your backyard. Maybe you'd like an indoor garden near a window in your home. Before you plant even one seed, do what successful gardeners do: make a sun chart.

4   A sun chart shows you how much sun a place gets. This is called *sun exposure*. Different plants need different amounts of sun exposure. A sun chart will give you a head start on bringing your dream garden to life.

Prepare Your Chart

5   On a large sheet of paper, make a chart like the one shown below. Across the top, write the hours from 8 a.m. to 8 p.m. Then plan a day to complete the chart. Pick a nice sunny day in the late spring or early summer. It should be a day when you are home near your garden spot most of the day.

8 A.M.	9 A.M.	10 A.M.	11 A.M.	12 P.M.	1 P.M.	2 P.M.	3 P.M.	4 P.M.	5 P.M.	6 P.M.	7 P.M.	8 P.M.

Complete Your Chart

6   On your chart-making day, get up early! Around eight o'clock, check your garden spot. Is the sun shining on it? Is it in the shade? Or is there a little of both, perhaps with some sun <u>filtering</u> through leaves? This is called *partial sun* or *partial shade.* Fill in the first box on your sun chart. Write "sun," "shade," "partial sun," or "partial shade."

7   Check the garden spot every hour and note the amount of sun. Keep careful notes on your chart. By 8 p.m., your chart will be complete.

8   Now look at your sun-exposure chart. You've collected a lot of information! Count the number of hours of sunlight. Now you know how many hours of sunlight your garden will get each day. That will help you choose the best plants for your garden space.

Choose Your Plants

9   When you choose a plant, read the tag. When you choose seeds, read the package. You'll find out if the plant's needs for sun exposure match the conditions in your garden. Some plants need full sun. Some do best with partial sun or partial shade. Others thrive in shade or mostly shade.

10   Have fun choosing the right kinds of plants for your garden spot. And have fun gardening!

More on Choosing Plants

11   First, make your sun-exposure chart. Next, add up the hours of sunlight. You'll need to read each plant's tag, too. Then use this guide to choose your plants.

12   Your garden gets at least 6 hours of sun. Choose plants that need FULL SUN.

13   Your garden gets 3 to 6 hours of sunlight. Choose plants that need PARTIAL SUN or PARTIAL SHADE.

14   Your garden gets fewer than 3 hours of sun each day. Choose plants that need SHADE.

Sun Charts
The Secret to Great Gardens

Remember to take notes! →

1   It feels so good when you're out in the sunshine. Since sunlight gives your body vitamin D, it's also good for you. However, excessive sunlight can cause burns and even serious illness. It's important for people to get some sun, just not too much.

2   What's true for people also holds true for plants. Plants are healthiest when they receive the optimum amount of sunlight—not too much, and not too little. In fact, the biggest secret to growing a great garden is to make sure that your plants get the right amount of sun.

3   Would you like to plant a garden? Maybe you have a little space in your backyard where you can start a garden. Or perhaps you'd like to plant an indoor garden near a window in your home. However, before you plant even a single seed, you should do what successful gardeners do: make a sun chart.

4   A sun chart shows you how much sun your location receives throughout the day. This is called *sun exposure*. Different plants need different amounts of sun exposure, and a sun chart will give you a head start on bringing your dream garden to life.

Prepare Your Chart

5   On a large sheet of paper, make a chart like the one shown below. Across the top, write the hours from 8 a.m. to 8 p.m. Then plan a day that you can devote to completing the chart. You'll want to select a nice sunny day in the late spring or early summer. Ideally, it should be a time when you are home near your garden spot for most of the day.

8 A.M.	9 A.M.	10 A.M.	11 A.M.	12 P.M.	1 P.M.	2 P.M.	3 P.M.	4 P.M.	5 P.M.	6 P.M.	7 P.M.	8 P.M.

MY STAR READER • GRADE 4 • ©2016 BENCHMARK EDUCATION COMPANY, LLC

Complete Your Chart

6   On your chart-making day, get up early in the morning! Around eight o'clock, check the sun exposure on your garden spot. Is the sun shining on your garden? Or is the garden in complete shade? Or is there a little of both sun and shade, perhaps with some sun <u>filtering</u> through leaves? This is called *partial sun* or *partial shade*. Fill in the first box on your sun chart, writing "sun," "shade," "partial sun," or "partial shade."

7   Every hour, you should check your garden spot, taking note of the amount of sun you see. Keep careful notes on your chart. By 8 p.m., your chart will be complete.

8   Now look at your sun-exposure chart. You should have collected a lot of information about sun exposure during the day. Count up the number of hours of sunlight. Now you know how many hours of sunlight your garden will get each day. That will help you choose the best plants for your garden space.

Choose Your Plants

9   When you choose a plant, be sure to read the tag. Likewise, be sure to read the package when you choose seeds to plant. From the package, you'll find out if the plant's needs for sun exposure match the conditions in your garden. Some plants need full sun. Some do best with partial sun or partial shade. Others thrive in shade or mostly shade.

10   Have fun choosing the right kinds of plants for your garden spot. And have fun gardening!

More on Choosing Plants

11   First, make your sun-exposure chart. Next, add up the hours of sunlight. You'll need to read each plant's tag too. Then use this guide to choose your plants.

12   Your garden gets at least 6 hours of sun. Choose plants that need FULL SUN.

13   Your garden gets 3 to 6 hours of sunlight. Choose plants that need PARTIAL SUN or PARTIAL SHADE.

14   Your garden gets fewer than 3 hours of sun each day. Choose plants that need SHADE.

Notes:

Text Evidence Questions

1. Why does the author include the picture of the blank sun chart?

_____

Text Evidence:

_____

_____

2. Why are the pictures of the flowerpots useful for the reader?

_____

_____

Text Evidence:

_____

_____

3. What does the author say someone should do before choosing plants for a garden?

_____

_____

Text Evidence:

_____

_____

_____

4. What is the main idea of the section "More on Choosing Plants"?

_____

_____

Text Evidence:

_____

_____

_____

MY STAR READER • GRADE 4 • ©2016 BENCHMARK EDUCATION COMPANY, LLC

Assessment Practice Questions

1. **Part A**

   Look up the word <u>filter</u> in a dictionary. Which option **best** describes what is happening to the sun when it is "<u>filtering</u> through leaves" in paragraph 6?

   A. Only a little sun is going through the leaves.

   B. The sunlight is being put through a machine of some kind.

   C. The leaves are removing something from the sunlight.

   D. Someone is taking a picture of the sun in black and white.

1. **Part B**

   Using context clues, which word in paragraph 6 **best** helps the reader understand the meaning of the word <u>filtering</u>?

   A. partial

   B. garden

   C. shining

   D. leaves

   _____

2. What is the purpose of creating a sun chart? How does it help gardeners?

   _____

   _____

   _____

Writing

The first part of "How to Build a Japanese Fighter Kite" describes what skills are needed to fly this special kind of kite. Pretend you are practicing flying a fighter kite. Tell what happens as you begin to fly the kite and how things change the more practice you have. Be sure to tell how you feel as you learn this new skill. Use text evidence to help you tell what you try to do as you fly your kite. Complete the rest of the chart to organize your writing by listing the ideas in sequence.

Sequence of Events:
First
Second
Third
Fourth

Digging Deeper into Identifying Sequence of Events

Use paragraphs 7, 8, and 9 of "How to Build a Japanese Fighter Kite" to complete the chart that shows one part of the process in building the kite.

Step 1	Text Evidence:
Step 2	**Text Evidence:**
Step 3	**Text Evidence:**

Poetry

What is a poem?

A poem is an arrangement of words that uses imagery and rhythm to capture a moment in time and share a feeling. The lines of most poems are arranged in paragraphs called *stanzas*. Poems may or may not rhyme, and don't always follow punctuation rules.

What is the purpose of a poem?

The purpose of a poem is to tell a story or capture a thought, image, sound, or feeling in a short way.

How do you read a poem?

Read the title. Then read each line and try to find the rhythm of the poem. Think about what each idea adds to the picture the poet, or speaker, is "painting." Try to visualize the images, sounds, and feelings that the poet describes.

Think about the poem's theme and how it makes you feel. Read the poem again and look deeper to find hidden or double meanings.

Who invented poems?

People have shared poems for thousands of years. In ancient days, poems were used to tell stories.

It is often short.

Uses imagery to capture a moment, tell a story, or convey an emotion.

It has rhythm.

Features of a
Poem

Lines can be rhymed or unrhymed.

Lines can be a word, a phrase, or a full sentence.

Lines in a poem can be grouped to form a stanza.

Poetry

Remember to annotate the text as you read!

from

Rain in Summer

by Henry Wadsworth Longfellow

How beautiful is the rain!
After the dust and heat,
In the broad and fiery street,
In the narrow lane,
5   How beautiful is the rain!

How it clatters along the roofs,
Like the tramp of hoofs.
How it gushes and struggles out
From the throat of the overflowing spout!

10 Across the window-pane
It pours and pours;
And swift and wide
With a muddy tide,
Like a river down the gutter roars
15 The rain, the welcome rain!

The sick man from his chamber looks
At the twisted brooks;
He can feel the cool
Breath of each little pool;

Notes:

20 His fevered brain
Grows calm again,
And he breathes a blessing on the rain.

From the neighboring school
Come the boys,
25 With more than their wonted noise
And commotion;
And down the wet streets
Sail their mimic fleets,
Till the treacherous pool
30 Ingulfs them in its whirling
And turbulent ocean.

In the country, on every side,
Where far and wide,
Like a leopard's tawny and spotted hide,
35 Stretches the plain,
To the dry grass and the drier grain.
How welcome is the rain! . . .

Poetry

Remember to jot down your thinking!

The Rainy Morning

by James Whitcomb Riley

The dawn of the day was dreary,
And the lowering clouds o'erhead
Wept in a silent sorrow
Where the sweet sunshine lay dead;
5 And a wind came out of the eastward
Like an endless sigh of pain,
And the leaves fell down in the pathway
And writhed in the falling rain.

I had tried in a brave endeavor
10 To chord my harp with the sun,
But the strings would slacken ever,
And the task was a weary one:
And so, like a child impatient
And sick of a <u>discontent</u>,
15 I bowed in a shower of teardrops
And mourned with the instrument.

And lo! as I bowed, the splendor
Of the sun bent over me,
With a touch as warm and tender
20 As a father's hand might be:
And even as I felt its presence,
My clouded soul grew bright,
And the tears, like the rain of morning,
Melted in mists of light.

MY STAR READER • GRADE 4 • ©2016 BENCHMARK EDUCATION COMPANY, LLC

MY STAR READER • GRADE 4 • ©2016 BENCHMARK EDUCATION COMPANY, LLC

Poetry

Find Text Evidence to Analyze Sensory Language

Text Evidence from "Rain in Summer"	Type of Sensory Language	Meaning

Find Text Evidence to Summarize the Text

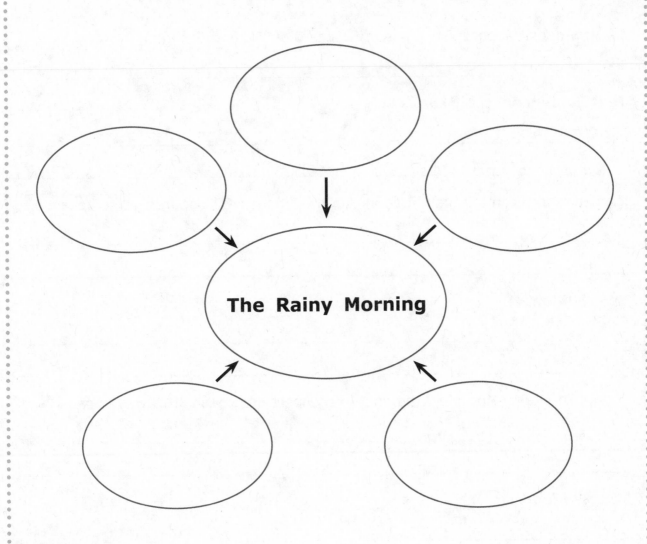

The Rainy Morning

Summary

_____

_____

_____

_____

_____

_____

Text Evidence Questions

1. How does the poet use simile in Stanza 2 of "Rain in Summer"?

_____

Text Evidence:

_____

_____

2. The reader can tell that "Rain in Summer" does NOT use free verse because—

_____

_____

Text Evidence:

_____

_____

3. In "The Rainy Morning," the poet likely spells "o'erhead" this way because —

_____

_____

Text Evidence:

_____

_____

4. Why does the poet use the words "And lo!" in Stanza 3 of "The Rainy Morning"?

_____

_____

Text Evidence:

_____

_____

MY STAR READER • GRADE 4 • ©2016 BENCHMARK EDUCATION COMPANY, LLC

Assessment Practice Questions

1. How does the speaker in the poem "Rain in Summer" feel about the rain? Use examples from the passage to support your answer.

_____

_____

_____

_____

_____

2. **Part A**

Look at the poem "The Rainy Morning." Use a dictionary. Which dictionary entry for <u>discontent</u> in line 14 is **most likely** the correct choice?

A. verb, "to make dissatisfied or displeased"

B. noun, "uneasiness of mind"

C. adjective, "expressing or showing lack of satisfaction"

D. none of the above

2. **Part B**

Look at the poem "Rain in Summer." Which line **best** fits the definition of <u>discontent</u> in part A?

A. Line 30

B. Line 1

C. Line 25

D. Line 20

Highlight important information!

Undersea

by Marchette Chute

Beneath the waters
Green and cool
The mermaids keep
A swimming school.
5   The oysters trot;
The lobsters prance;
The dolphins come
To join the dance.
But the jellyfish
10   Who are rather small
Can't seem to learn
The steps at all.

Dreamscape

by Lillian M. Fisher

Remember
to annotate!
←

A giant came into my dream
And thundered to and fro.
As thunder-lizards often do
He traveled high and low.
5 He shook the hills and mountaintops
And spilled the seven seas.
He drank eleven rivers,
He ate a hundred trees.
But even thunder-giants sleep—
10 He wandered off to find his bed.
I didn't notice where he went,
I simply, quickly, woke instead!

Text Evidence Questions

1. What is swimming being compared to in the poem "Undersea"?

_____

Text Evidence:

_____

2. Which sea creature mentioned in the poem cannot keep up with the rest?

_____

_____

Text Evidence:

_____

_____

3. How can you tell that this poem is a work of fiction?

_____

_____

_____

Text Evidence:

_____

_____

4. Describe the setting for this poem. What kind of environment is it?

_____

_____

Text Evidence:

_____

_____

Assessment Practice Questions

1. What is this poem **most likely** about?

   A. why jellyfish cannot swim

   B. what mermaids like to do for work

   C. different sea animals learning how to swim

   D. dolphins dancing

   _____

2. Jellyfish do not have a skeletal system (bones and muscle). They propel themselves by squirting water from their mouths. Jellyfish do not really swim. Instead, they drift in the water. Looking back at the poem, which lines **best** reflect these facts, and why?

   _____

   _____

   _____

   _____

   _____

3. What reason(s) **best** explains why this is a poem? Choose all that apply.

   A. There is a rhythm.

   B. The poem is fiction.

   C. The title of the poem is one word.

   D. Some or all of the lines rhyme.

Writing

Both poems are about rain, but they are different in many ways, too. Complete the chart. Then write a paragraph on the lines below to explain how one poet's mood and attitude about rain is different from the other.

Rain in Summer	The Rainy Morning

_____

_____

_____

_____

_____

_____

_____

_____

Vocabulary

Define each word related to poetry. Give an example of each from "Rain in Summer" or "The Rainy Morning."

1. rhyme

meaning: _____

_____

example: _____

_____

2. stanza

meaning: _____

_____

example: _____

_____

_____

3. line break

meaning: _____

example: _____

Write an example from "Rain in Summer" or "The Rainy Morning" that shows two rhyming lines followed by another two rhyming lines.

_____

_____

_____

_____

Informational Texts:
Social Studies

What is an informational text?

Informational texts present nonfiction information in an accurate and organized way. They are often about a single subject such as an event or time period in history. They may be about any topic, such as an annual event or a hobby. A newspaper account of a local election and a history book chapter on a famous battle are examples of informational texts.

What is the purpose of an informational text?

Informational texts have one main purpose: to inform. The best informational writing does this in a way that keeps readers' attention. It pulls readers in, making them want to keep reading and learn more about the topic.

How do you read an informational text?

Look for facts and the details that support them. Read critically to make sure conclusions make sense. If there are different ways to look at an event or situation, make sure they are given. Ask yourself: *What did I learn from this text? What conclusions can I draw from what I have read?*

Who writes informational texts?

Writers who know their topic well write good informational texts. They make sure that they support the information in their work with historical facts, graphics like time lines and diagrams, and expert evidence. They provide more than one person's point of view. They use primary sources, firsthand information, such as journals and photographs.

The information is accurate, and the facts have been checked.

The text has a strong beginning that "hooks" the reader.

The text uses primary sources when appropriate.

Features of an Informational Text: *Social Studies*

The information includes graphics that support the text.

The text has a strong ending that keeps readers thinking.

The text includes multiple perspectives so that a reader can draw his or her own conclusions.

The text has a logical organization of major concepts.

My Star Reader • Grade 4 • ©2016 Benchmark Education Company, LLC

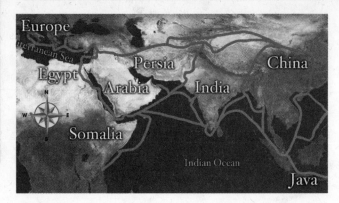

The Silk Road

Remember to highlight important information! →

1   The world's first great trade route was the Silk Road. It was a network of roads and trails stretching thousands of miles across Asia. Branches of the Silk Road passed through mountain ranges, deserts, and broad grasslands. Over time, these paths linked the great cities of the Middle East to faraway China.

2   The Silk Road didn't spring up overnight. It developed over hundreds and hundreds of years. Small trails connected, producing longer trails. Traders journeyed along these varied paths to buy and sell their goods. As trade grew, new trails and new roads became connected to the Silk Road, and the trade route expanded.

Tough Travel

3   A journey on the Silk Road could be difficult, dangerous, and slow. Trails passed through sandy deserts and harsh mountain passes. Many traders traveled in caravans for safety. Merchants and guards, missionaries and pilgrims trekked together on the road. Going with a group gave some protection from bandits and soldiers.

4   The main pack animals were camels. They could go long distances without water and live on shrubs and thorny bushes. They could also carry huge loads, up to 500 pounds. But these sturdy animals only covered about thirty miles per day.

Varied Goods

5   The name Silk Road highlights the most important good sold along the route: Chinese silk. Demand for this commodity made silk very valuable, and people traveled thousands of miles to get it. Outside of China, nobody

knew how to produce silk. Chinese officials tried to keep silk production a secret. Eventually, spies discovered that silk comes from the caterpillars of the silkworm moth. The caterpillars eat the leaves of mulberry trees and spin cocoons that can be made into silk products. In time, people began to make silk in other lands.

6   Many other goods moved along the Silk Road from many different places. Caravans and camels transported spices, nuts, dates, tea, and other food products. Their loads also contained gold, precious stones, porcelain, and glassware. Merchants traded horses and cattle, as well.

Other Exchanges

7   Goods were not the only important exchanges that took place because of the Silk Road. Travelers entertained each other, traded ideas, and swapped information along the road. They shared stories, music, art, and dance. These art forms, like trade goods, passed from place to place. Sometimes tales, music, and art changed in new settings or mingled with local arts.

8   Similarly, travelers traded new skills, tools, and inventions. They shared new methods for farming and fighting. Paper money, compasses, and gunpowder, for example, were all Chinese inventions. People who traveled to China surely brought some of these ideas and products back with them.

9   Religion was also transmitted from traveler to traveler along the Silk Road. Buddhism started in India and spread across China and into central Asia. Later, Islam traveled across northern Africa into Central Asia by way of the trade routes.

Endings and Beginnings

10   By the late 1400s, trade was declining on the Silk Road. Explorers from Europe, such as Christopher Columbus, began to search for better and faster sea routes to Asia. Eventually, new maritime routes replaced the great land route, and the Silk Road faded away.

Notes:

Sailing to Asia

▲ *Vasco da Gama Leaving Portugal,* **mural by John Henry Amshewitz**

Remember to take notes! →

1   Does the name Marco Polo sound familiar? He is one of the most famous explorers in history. In the early 1300s, he became one of the first Europeans to travel across the lands stretching from Italy to China. He played an important role in the establishment of the Silk Road. But there is another important European explorer you may not know about: Vasco da Gama. What Marco Polo accomplished on foot, da Gama accomplished on water. Vasco da Gama was the first explorer to sail from Europe to India.

2   The Silk Road helped merchants trade goods between European, Middle Eastern, and Asian nations. But the Silk Road was a long and dangerous route. There were mountains to climb, deserts to cross, and bandits to avoid. Camels were used to carry goods, and this limited the amount a merchant could trade. Leaders in many nations longed for an ocean route that would make trading easier.

Notes:

3   On July 8, 1497, Vasco da Gama and his crew left Lisbon, Portugal, in four ships. They sailed south around Africa's Cape of Good Hope and then northward toward India. On May 20, 1498, da Gama arrived in Calicut, India. He and his crew were the first Europeans to sail all the way to Asia! By doing so, da Gama proved that Europeans could reach Asia by sailing around Africa. His next goal was to build a trade station for Portugal in India.

▲ **Vasco da Gama, c. 1460–1524 by António Manuel da Fonseca (1796–1890)**

4   At first, the people of India welcomed da Gama and his men with celebrations and feasts. But this friendliness did not last long. The Hindu king feared that if he allowed Portugal to build a trade station, he would anger merchants from other countries. So he refused. Da Gama was disappointed, but what could he do? He decided to lead his men back home.

5   When da Gama arrived back in Portugal, he received a hero's welcome. The king rewarded him with money and made him an admiral. Da Gama had learned a lot during the trip and wanted to try again. In February of 1502, da Gama set sail for India as a viceroy for the king of Portugal. As an official representative of the king, he was finally allowed to build a trade center. An ocean trade route between Europe and Asia was established.

6   After da Gama's successful voyages, many other countries followed suit. People throughout Europe, Africa, and Asia benefited greatly from this trade and exploration. Goods, technologies, and ideas spread to more areas and at a faster rate than along the Silk Road. The world was changed forever. Da Gama and Marco Polo may have taken different paths, but both changed the world in <u>astounding</u> ways.

Find Text Evidence to Understand Text Features

Tough Travel	
Varied Goods	
Other Exchanges	
Endings and Beginnings	

Find Text Evidence to Summarize the Text

Events

Summary

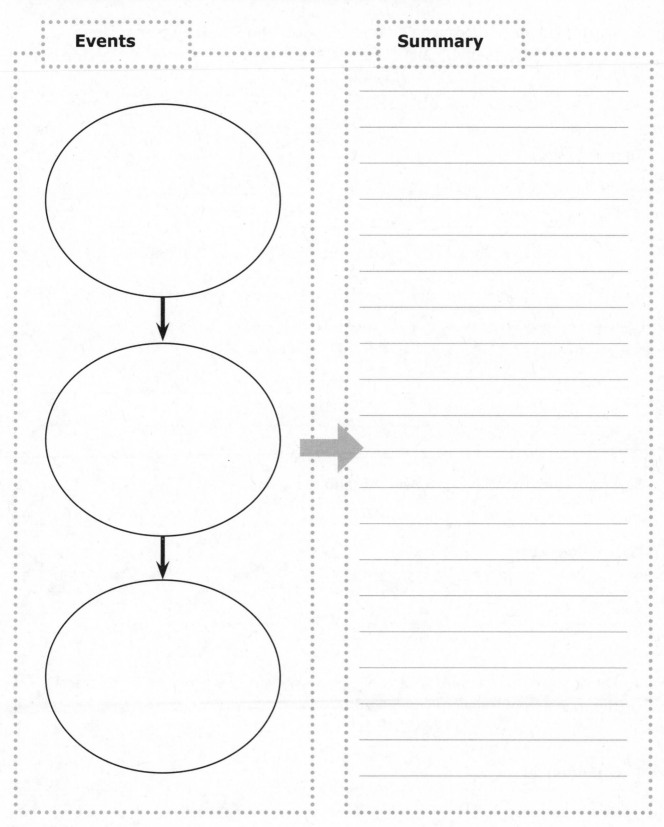

Independent **Workstation** ⭐ **1**

Text Evidence Questions

1. What does the author mean by the sentence "The Silk Road didn't spring up overnight," in paragraph 2 of "The Silk Road"?

_____

_____

Text Evidence:

_____

_____

2. What is the main idea of the section "Varied Goods" in "The Silk Road"?

_____

_____

Text Evidence:

_____

_____

_____

3. How is the text "Sailing to Asia" organized?

_____

Text Evidence:

_____

_____

_____

4. Which word in paragraph 2 of "Sailing to Asia" helps the reader understand the meaning of the word "merchant"?

_____

Text Evidence:

_____

_____

Assessment Practice Questions

1. Which of these is the **best** summary of "The Silk Road"?

    A. Chinese silk was a very valuable product along the Silk Road.

    B. The Silk Road was a trade route for goods, ideas, culture, and information.

    C. Religion such as Buddhism and Islam were spread along the Silk Road.

    D. The Silk Road was no longer needed after ocean travel improved.

2. Which area on the map is **not** part of the Silk Road?

    A. China

    B. Persia

    C. India

    D. Somalia

3. Look at the word <u>astounding</u> in paragraph 6 of "Sailing to Asia." Using context clues from the passage, what do you think this word **most likely** means?

    _____

    _____

    _____

    _____

Native American Tribes of Georgia

Remember to take notes! →

1   Native Americans were living in America before Columbus came. Native Americans had settled across the country. They farmed and hunted. They set up villages in the wilderness. Two large tribes lived in the southeast. These were the Cherokee and the Creek.

2   The Cherokee tribe lived in what is, today, Georgia and Alabama. They covered an area of 100,000 square miles! The Cherokee tribe grew very large. That's because it invited other people to join them. Native Americans from other tribes joined the Cherokee. European settlers were also welcome. So were former slaves. The Cherokee Nation had seven different clans. Each clan had a different job. The Aniwaya, or "Wolf Clan," was the army. The "Paint Clan" (Aniwodi) were doctors. The "Deer Clan" (Anikawi) were fast runners and hunters.

3   The Cherokee mostly stayed in one place. They lived in houses made of mud and clay. Their clothing was

Notes:

made from animal skin. Unlike many tribes, they had a written language. A man named Sequoyah was a Cherokee silversmith. He developed a syllabary. The syllabary included 84 to 86 different syllables. These syllables were used to make up Cherokee words.

4   The Creek tribe was also very large. It had the most people of any Georgian tribe until the 1760s. The tribe's name came from English settlers. The English called them "the Creek" because the tribe lived near Ochese Creek. The name stuck. The Creek were friendly to the settlers. They even helped them establish a colony in Savannah. The Creek were skilled hunters. They traded deerskins for metal and cloth. Like the Cherokee, the Creek invited outsiders to become citizens of their tribe.

5   The Creek made their houses out of grass or river cane. River cane is a kind of bamboo. They made clothing from plants or animal skins. Even bark was used to make clothing! Like the Cherokee tribes, they had clans, including the Bear, Deer, and Fish.

6   In the 1800s, the Creek and Cherokee were forced off their lands. Many Native Americans traveled west. They went to Oklahoma, where they continued their traditions. Today, the state government recognizes the Creek and Cherokee as the only American Indian tribes of Georgia.

First Settlers of Savannah

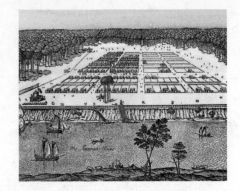

1   On a chilly morning in November of 1732, 114 people boarded a ship in England. The ship was called the *Anne*. The group included men, women, and children. They were sailing to America to found a new colony. The colony would be called Georgia.

2   Almost two months later, in 1733, they landed in South Carolina. That was not their final stop. First, their leader, James Edward Oglethorpe, had work to do. He had to find a good home for the colonists.

3   Oglethorpe traveled south along the coast. He found an ideal place. Other countries such as Spain wanted this land. That's why Oglethorpe chose a place on a hill. It was called Yamacraw Bluff. Being up high would protect the colonists from attack. Also, the site was surrounded by swamps that would slow down any attackers.

4   Next, Oglethorpe made peace with the local Native Americans. He asked a woman named Mary Musgrove to help. A Creek woman, she was married to an Englishman named John Musgrove. She introduced Oglethorpe to the Creek leader, Tomochichi. Together, they came to an agreement. Then Oglethorpe went back to South Carolina for the colonists.

5   The colonists came to their new home on February 1, 1733. They set up tents. These would protect them from the weather. Then they cleared trees. They called their new home Savannah.

6   The settlers of Savannah had a huge job. First, they had to build a stockade to protect the town. This strong fence was made with logs. Then they had to build homes for everyone. When spring came, they planted crops.

Notes:

7   Savannah was the first planned city in America. That means people designed the city before it was built. The plan was to divide the city into twenty-four parts. Each part would have a square in the center. These squares would be places where people could meet. By 1734, four of these squares had been built.

8   These first colonists had many different skills. There were tailors, gardeners, and carpenters. There was one wheelwright, potash makers, a turner, a miller, and a baker. There were also mercers who planned to sell silk. Silk was a popular fabric, but it was very expensive. Silk is made by the caterpillars of the silkworm moth. The worms feed on the leaves of the mulberry tree. The British thought the weather in Georgia would be perfect for growing mulberry trees. They thought silk would become a big business.

9   However, the colonists ran into problems. Not everyone liked the work. Not everyone liked to farm. The silkworm caterpillars did not grow well in Georgia. The silk industry was not a big success.

10   There were other problems, too, for the colonists. Insects from the swamps carried diseases. People became sick. In the first year, many colonists died. Others left Georgia and went back to South Carolina. The living was easier there.

11   Over the next few years, more settlers came to Savannah. The climate was good for cotton. Farmers decided to grow cotton instead of making silk. Some of the people made a lot of money from farming. They began to build fancy homes near the town squares. Savannah became a nice place to live.

12   If you visit Savannah today, you'll see twenty-one of those original squares. You'll see streets shaded by oak trees. You'll see grand homes. You can even stand on Yamacraw Bluff. You can picture what it was like long ago. You can think about the first people who settled the city.

Native American Tribes of Georgia

1   Long before Columbus reached America, Native Americans were settling across the country. They farmed, hunted, and carved out villages in the wilderness. In the southeast, there were two large Native American tribes: the Cherokee and the Creek.

2   The Cherokee tribe was spread out across what is, today, Georgia and Alabama. In total, it took up an area of 100,000 square miles! The Cherokee tribe grew so large because it invited other people to join them. Native Americans from other tribes, European settlers, and former slaves were welcome in the Cherokee Nation. Within the Cherokee Nation there were seven different clans, and each clan had a different job. The Aniwaya, or "Wolf Clan," for example, served as the army. The "Paint Clan" (Aniwodi) served as doctors. The "Deer Clan" (Anikawi) could run very fast and were skilled hunters.

3   The Cherokee were not nomadic hunters. They mostly stayed in one place. They lived in houses made of mud and clay and wore clothing made from

Notes:

animal skin. One thing they had that many tribes did not was a written language. A man named Sequoyah was a Cherokee silversmith who developed a syllabary. Unlike the alphabet, the syllabary was a collection of between 84 to 86 different syllables. These syllables were rearranged to make up Cherokee words.

4   The Creek tribe had the largest population of any tribe in Georgia until the 1760s. The tribe's name came from English settlers living in South Carolina who often traded with them. Since the Native Americans lived near the Ochese Creek, the settlers called them "the Creek." The name stuck. The Creek tribe was friendly to the English colonists. They even helped them establish a colony in Savannah. Savannah later became the first state capital of Georgia. The Creek were skilled hunters and traded deerskins for metal, cloth, and other textiles. Like the Cherokee, the Creek invited outsiders to become citizens of their tribe.

5   The Creek lived in houses made out of grass or river cane, which is a kind of bamboo. Before Western influence, they wore clothing fashioned from plants or animal hides. Even bark was used to make clothing! Similar to the Cherokee tribes, they too had clans, including Bear, Deer, and Fish.

6   Sadly, the Creek and Cherokee tribes were forced off of their land in the 1800s. Many Native Americans traveled west to Oklahoma and continued their traditions there. Today, the state government recognizes the Creek and Cherokee as the only American Indian tribes of Georgia.

First Settlers of Savannah

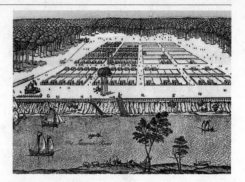

Remember to take notes!

1   On a chilly morning in November of 1732, 114 people boarded a ship in England called the *Anne*. The group included men, women, and children. They were embarking on an adventure that would change their lives. They were sailing to America to found the new colony of Georgia.

2   Almost two months later, in 1733, they arrived in South Carolina. However, that was not their final stop. Their leader, James Edward Oglethorpe, had work to do first. He traveled south along the coast to find a good home for the colonists.

3   Oglethorpe found an ideal place for the settlement. Other countries such as Spain wanted this land, so Oglethorpe chose a place on a hill. It was called Yamacraw Bluff. Being up high would protect the colonists from attack. Also, the site was surrounded by swamps, which would slow down any attackers.

4   Next, Oglethorpe made peace with the Native Americans in the area. He asked a woman named Mary Musgrove to help. She was a Creek woman married to an Englishman named John Musgrove. She introduced Oglethorpe to the Creek leader, Tomochichi, and they reached an agreement. Then Oglethorpe went back to South Carolina to gather his colonists.

5   The colonists arrived at their new home on February 1, 1733. They set up tents that would protect them from the weather. Then they began to clear trees for a home they called Savannah.

6   The settlers of Savannah had a huge job to do. First, they had to build a stockade to protect the town. This strong fence was made with logs. Then the settlers had to build homes for everyone. When spring came, they planted crops.

Notes:

7   Savannah was the first planned city in America. That means people designed the city before it was built. The plan divided the city into twenty-four parts. Each part would have a square in the center. These squares would be meeting places for merchants and neighbors. By 1734, four of these squares had been built.

8   These first colonists had many different skills. There were tailors, gardeners, and carpenters. There was one wheelwright, potash makers, a turner, a miller, and a baker. There were also mercers who planned to sell silk. Silk was a popular fabric at the time, but it was very expensive. Silk is produced by the caterpillars of the silkworm moth, which feed on the leaves of the mulberry tree. The British believed that the climate in Georgia was perfect for growing mulberry trees and developing a silk industry. So the colonists began to grow mulberry trees.

9   However, not everyone was suited to the hard work. Not everyone liked to farm. The silkworm caterpillars did not grow well in the Georgia climate, so silk production was not a great success.

10   Disease-carrying insects from the swamps bit the colonists, and many became sick. In the first year, many colonists died. Others left Georgia and went back to South Carolina, where the living was easier.

11   Despite the hardships, more people arrived in Savannah in the next few years. The climate was great for cotton, and the farmers began growing it instead of trying to make silk. Some of the people made fortunes from selling cotton and other crops. They began to build fancy homes near the town squares. Savannah became a nice place to live.

12   Today, you can visit Savannah and see twenty-one of the original squares. You can walk along the streets shaded by oak trees and see the grand homes. You can stand on Yamacraw Bluff. With a little imagination, you can picture what it was like for the first people who settled in this beautiful place.

Text Evidence Questions

1. Is the first sentence of paragraph 2 in "Native American Tribes of Georgia" a fact or opinion? Explain how you can tell.

_____

Text Evidence:

_____

2. What is the author's purpose for writing the selection "Native American Tribes of Georgia"?

_____

Text Evidence:

_____

_____

_____

3. According to "First Settlers of Savannah," why did the settlers' plan to sell silk not succeed?

_____

Text Evidence:

_____

_____

4. What made Georgia a successful place to live, according to "First Settlers of Savannah"?

_____

Text Evidence:

_____

_____

Assessment Practice Questions

1. Why do you think these two texts were placed together? What connects them? Use examples from the passages to support your answer.

_____

_____

_____

_____

2. Part A

In "Native American Tribes of Georgia," what **best** describes the Cherokee and Creek tribes?

A. They were isolated tribes that specialized in fighting.

B. They were the same tribe; "Creek" is a nickname for Cherokee.

C. They were friendly, skillful tribes and encouraged outsiders to join.

D. They were friendly to outsiders but refused to trade with them.

2. Part B

Based on your answer to part A, explain how this not only helped the Cherokee and Creek tribes, but also the settlers of Georgia. Use examples from the passage to support your answer.

_____

_____

_____

_____

_____

Writing

"The Silk Road" and "Sailing to Asia" are both informational texts. Compare and contrast how the subjects of the texts are alike and different. Use the Venn diagram to help you organize your ideas. Then write a paragraph to explain your answer on the lines.

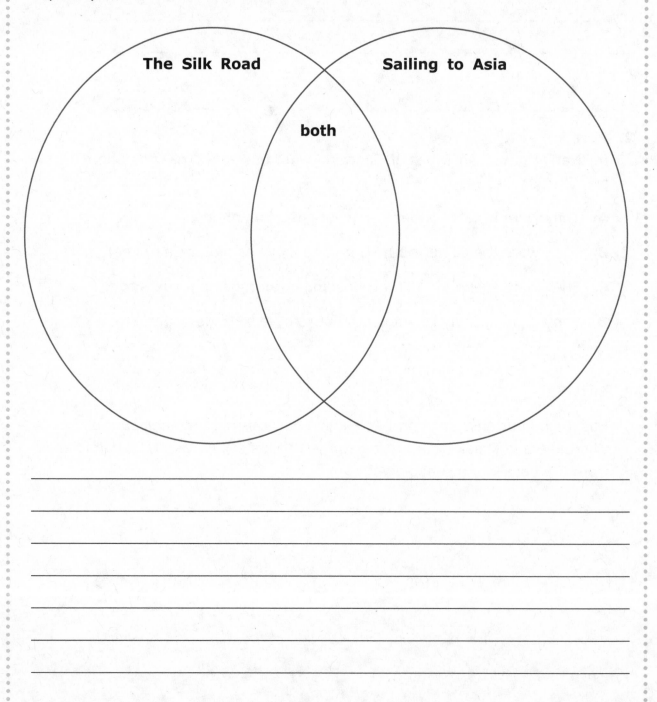

The Silk Road   **Sailing to Asia**

both

_____

_____

_____

_____

_____

_____

_____

MY STAR READER • GRADE 4 • ©2016 BENCHMARK EDUCATION COMPANY, LLC

Vocabulary

Review the words from "The Silk Road" below. Think about categories that you can sort the words into. Name the categories in the boxes below. Then sort the words into the categories.

Africa	**Asia**	**China**	**dangerous**
Europe	**glassware**	**gold**	**harsh**
porcelain	**sandy**	**silk**	**Silk Road**
spices	**thorny**	**trails**	**varied**

Category 1	Category 2	Category 3

DRAMA

What is a drama?

A drama is a story written in script form. The main goal is for the script to be performed by actors in front of an audience. The events in a drama are shown in short sections called *scenes.* The scenes may be grouped into larger sections called *acts.* Many dramas are divided into two or three acts. Dramas consist almost entirely of dialogue (DY-uh-laug), or conversation between people.

What is the purpose of a drama?

A drama shows people in action. The main characters face a conflict or have a problem to solve. The purpose of a drama is to let the audience (or readers) connect with the characters in the story and experience their emotions.

How do you read a drama?

Pay attention to the dialogue. Nearly all of the information comes from what the characters say and do. Note when and where the story takes place. Use your imagination to "see" the settings and actions. Finally, there are notes to the actors, director, and designers of the play called *stage directions,* written within parentheses. As you read, you will find it helpful to picture who is talking, who is listening, who is onstage, and who is not.

Who invented dramas?

The ancient Greeks performed the earliest dramas (or plays). They came up with the idea of an actor who "plays at" being someone else. These early dramas influenced future authors of dramas, whom we call playwrights (*wright* means "maker").

MY STAR READER • GRADE 4 • ©2016 BENCHMARK EDUCATION COMPANY, LLC

FEATURES OF A DRAMA

Dramas are written to be performed by live actors, onstage.

Dramas usually have one or more main character(s) and additional minor characters.

Dramas are told through dialogue and characters' actions.

The plot is based on conflict—a problem for the character to solve or a decision to make.

Drama scripts include stage directions.

Dramas take place in one or more time frames and settings.

Dramas may be divided into scenes or acts.

My Star Reader • Grade 4 • ©2016 Benchmark Education Company, LLC

Drama

Remember to highlight important information! ↘

Heidi

Cast of Characters:

HEIDI: a girl from the mountains of Switzerland

CLARA: a twelve-year-old girl living in Frankfurt, Germany

GRANDMAMA: CLARA'S grandmother

PETER: HEIDI'S best friend at home in the mountains

SETTING:

1 [HEIDI *is living for a short time with her friend,* CLARA, *in Frankfurt. In this scene,* HEIDI *is sitting with* GRANDMAMA *in the living room of* CLARA'S *home. The two are looking at a book.* HEIDI *is bent over the book, eagerly looking at the illustrations. Suddenly, her eyes open wide with wonder and surprise, and she lets out a joyful scream.* HEIDI *places her hand upon an illustration showing a peaceful flock of sheep grazing in a beautiful green pasture, a kind-looking shepherd leaning on his crook beneath a tree.* HEIDI'S *eyes fill with tears, and her screams of delight suddenly turn to sobs of sorrow.*]

Notes:

2   **GRANDMAMA:** [*soothingly and lovingly*] Come, child, you must not cry. Did this remind you of something? Now stop, and I'll tell you the story tonight. There are lovely stories in this book that people can read and tell. Dry your tears now, darling, I must ask you something. Stand up now and look at me! Now we are merry again!

3   [HEIDI *continues to cry for some time.* GRANDMAMA *waits patiently, places an arm around* HEIDI'S *shoulders, and gives her time to stop crying.* HEIDI *slowly begins to calm down.*]

4   **GRANDMAMA:** [*kindly*] Now it's all over. Now we'll be merry again.

5   [HEIDI *finally stops crying and turns her tear-streaked face up toward* GRANDMAMA.]

6   **GRANDMAMA:** Tell me now how your lessons are going. What have you learnt, child?

7   **HEIDI:** [*quietly, as if ashamed*] Nothing, but I knew that I never could learn it.

8   **GRANDMAMA:** What is it that you can't learn?

9   **HEIDI:** [*quietly*] I can't learn to read; it is too hard.

Notes:

10 **GRANDMAMA:** [*looking surprised*] What next? Who gave you this information?

11 **HEIDI:** Peter told me, and he tried over and over again, but he could not do it, for it is too hard.

12 [GRANDMAMA *sighs. Her eyes and voice soften and she gently turns* HEIDI'S *face to hers so she can look* HEIDI *right in the eyes.*]

13 **GRANDMAMA:** Well, what kind of boy is he? Heidi, you must not believe what Peter tells you, but try for yourself. I am sure you had your thoughts elsewhere when Mr. Candidate showed you the letters.

14 **HEIDI:** [*sounding defeated as if she is resigned to her fate*] It's no use.

15 [HEIDI *listens attentively and begins to sit taller in* GRANDMAMA'S *arms. A small smile begins to form on her face and a glimmer of hope begins to flicker in her eyes.*]

16 **GRANDMAMA:** When you can read, I am going to give you this book. You have seen the shepherd in the green pasture, and then you'll be able to find out all the strange things that happen to him. Yes, you can hear the whole story, and what he does with his sheep and his goats. You would like to know, wouldn't you, Heidi?

17 [HEIDI's *eyes sparkle as she listens to* GRANDMAMA, *and her smile brightens her face like the sun. She places her arms around* GRANDMAMA'S *neck.*]

18 **HEIDI:** [*bubbling with excitement*] If only I could read already!

19 **GRANDMAMA:** [*laughing and hugging* HEIDI *in return*] It won't be long, I can see that. Come now and let us go to Clara.

20 [HEIDI *gently closes the book.* GRANDMAMA *slowly rises from her seat, takes* HEIDI'S *hand in hers, and they walk out of the room in search of* CLARA.]

21 [HEIDI'S *eyes fill with tears again and her chin starts to quiver.* GRANDMAMA *hugs* HEIDI *tighter and continues patiently.*]

22 **GRANDMAMA:** I am going to tell you something, Heidi. You have not learnt to read because you have believed what Peter said. You shall believe me now, and I prophesy that you will learn it in a very short time, as a great many other children do that are like you and not like Peter.

Drama

Find Text Evidence to Make Inferences

Text Evidence	
What I Know	
Inference	

MY STAR READER • GRADE 4 • ©2016 BENCHMARK EDUCATION COMPANY, LLC

Find Text Evidence to Summarize the Text

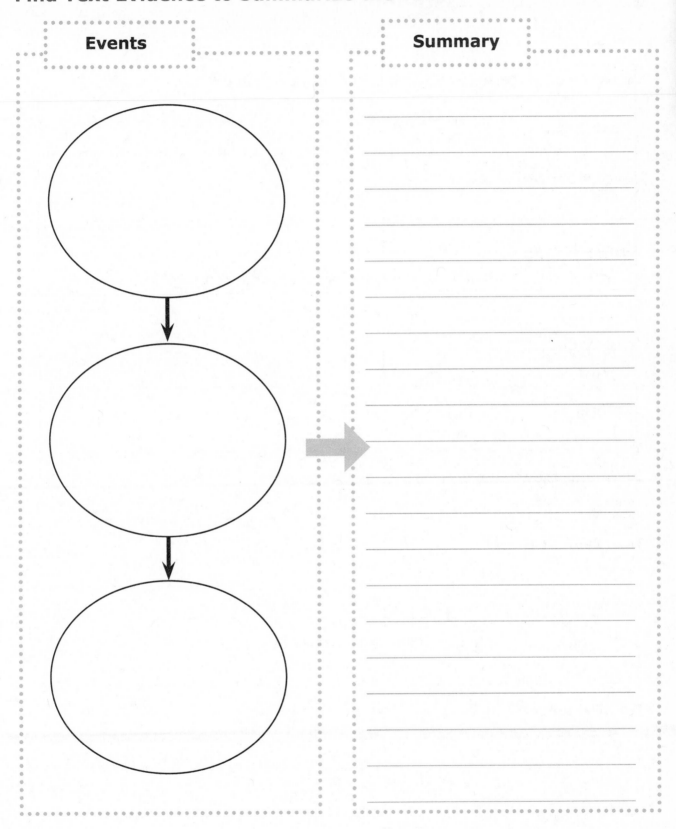

Events

Summary

Drama

Text Evidence Questions

1. Where does the story take place, and how can you tell?

_____

_____

Text Evidence:

_____

_____

2. How is the story similar to the story "A New World," on page 10?

_____

Text Evidence:

_____

_____

_____

3. What is the theme, or message, of the selection?

_____

Text Evidence:

_____

_____

4. In which paragraph does Heidi begin to feel better?

_____

Text Evidence:

_____

_____

_____

My Star Reader • Grade 4 • ©2016 Benchmark Education Company, LLC

Assessment Practice Questions

1. **Part A**

   What reason **most likely** explains why Heidi begins to cry at the beginning of the story?

   A. Heidi misses her home in Switzerland.

   B. The illustration scares her.

   C. She cannot read.

   D. She doesn't like sheep.

1. **Part B**

   Which line(s) from the passage **best** supports your answer to part A? Choose all that apply.

   A. Heidi: [*quietly, as if ashamed*] Nothing, but I knew that I never could learn it.

   B. Grandmama: [*kindly*] Now it's all over. Now we'll be merry again.

   C. Heidi: [*bubbling with excitement*] If only I could read already!

   D. Heidi: [*quietly*] I can't learn to read; it is too hard.

2. Look at the stage directions in your answers to part B. How do the stage directions help support your answer to part A?

   _____

   _____

   _____

   _____

Hurry, Linda

Highlight important information!

Cast of Characters:

BOOP: a well-meaning but nervous alarm clock
LINDA: an energetic girl, age ten, who likes to sleep late
LEFTY: a serious-minded red sock
RIGHTY: a fun-loving red sock

SETTING:

[*The stage is divided into three areas. At center stage, on a platform, is LINDA'S bedroom. To the right is the kitchen and a door leads offstage, to the outside. To the left is a hallway. The lights come up on the bedroom area. LINDA is sleeping soundly, snoring, when BOOP rings loudly.*]

1   **BOOP**: Boop, boop! 7 a.m. Time to get up.

2   **LINDA:** [*groans*] Already? Please can't I sleep some more?

3   **BOOP:** Well, you don't have to get up right this instant. I can wake you again in ten minutes.

4   **LINDA:** That sounds dreamy . . . Ten whole minutes more to saw wood in slumberland. But I really should get up. I've been late to school every day this week.

Notes:

Today, I want to be on time.

5 **BOOP:** What time do you need to leave?

6 **LINDA:** At 8:00 on the dot.

7 **BOOP:** That's 58 minutes, 12 seconds from now. You have plenty of time.

8 **LINDA:** No, I should get up now.

[LINDA *hops out of bed. She puts on her shirt. She puts on her jeans. She looks for her socks. She finds one red sock on the floor.*]

9 **LINDA:** Where's my other sock?

10 **LEFTY:** Don't play games, Righty. Linda wants to be on time today. We should help her.

11 **RIGHTY:** [*hiding under the bed*] I don't want to help. I want to play! Yoo-hoo, Linda. Come and find me.

[LINDA *looks in her closet. She looks behind her dresser.*]

12 **BOOP:** It's 7:10.

13 **LINDA:** Oh no! I'm going to be late again.

14 **LEFTY:** This isn't funny, Righty. Come out now!

15 **RIGHTY:** Here I am! But if you want me, you'll have to catch me.

[RIGHTY *shows himself.* LINDA *chases* RIGHTY *around her bedroom.*]

16 **LINDA:** Ha! I caught you! What time is it now, Boop?

17 **BOOP:** It's 7:15. Quarter past seven. Put on your socks, Linda, before they cause more trouble.

End Scene

Hurry, Linda

Cast of Characters:

BOOP: a well-meaning but nervous alarm clock

LINDA: an energetic girl, age ten, who likes to sleep late

LEFTY: a serious-minded red sock

RIGHTY: a fun-loving red sock

SWEET PUFFS: a box of sugary cereal

BRISTLES: a toothbrush

DOG: a dog

ZIP: a soft-sided zip-up lunch box

MOM

SCENE 2:

[*The lights in the bedroom fade out, then fade up in the kitchen area. LINDA, BOOP, LEFTY, and RIGHTY walk into the kitchen.*]

1   **BOOP:** Tick, tock, tick, tock. 7:45. Time is passing. Hurry, Linda! You still need to brush your teeth.

2   **ZIP:** Wait! She can't brush her teeth yet.

3   **SWEET PUFFS:** Why not? She's already eaten her breakfast.

4   **ZIP:** There's something she needs to do.

5   **DOG:** Play a game with me?

6   **ZIP:** No! She needs to make lunch!

7   **LINDA:** Hmmm . . . Mom usually makes my lunch . . .

8   **ZIP:** I'll help you. First, you make a sandwich. Peanut butter is easy. Then put some carrots and an apple inside me, too.

9   **BOOP:** [*very worried*] It's 7:50. There are only ten minutes left. Hurry, Linda, and brush your teeth.

10   **BRISTLES:** I've got the toothpaste ready for you. [*LINDA zips up her lunch box. Lights fade up on the hallway*

as LINDA, LEFTY, RIGHTY, *and* BRISTLES *run from the kitchen into the hallway area.* MOM *is standing there, sleepy-eyed.*]

11 **MOM:** Linda? What are you doing?

12 **LINDA:** I need to brush my teeth, Mom. Then I'll be ready to go.

13 **BRISTLES:** She'll be finished in two minutes, Mom.

14 [LINDA, RIGHTY, LEFTY, *and* BRISTLES *go offstage.*]

15 **MOM:** But, Linda . . .

16 **BOOP:** [*to* MOM] Linda did a good job today getting ready for school. She got up right away and got dressed.

17 **SWEET PUFFS:** She had her breakfast.

18 **ZIP:** She also made herself a healthful lunch.

19 **DOG:** And she took me for a walk.

20 **MOM:** Wow! Linda did all that? [LINDA, RIGHTY, LEFTY, *and* BRISTLES *return from the bathroom.*]

21 **BRISTLES:** Announcing Linda: ready for school!

22 **LEFTY:** What time is it, Boop?

23 **BOOP:** It's 7:55.

24 **LINDA:** Hooray! I'm not going to be late today!

25 **MOM:** That's wonderful, Linda. But . . .

26 **LINDA:** What's the matter, Mom? Did I forget to do something?

27 **MOM:** Not exactly, but . . .

28 **LINDA:** Then what is wrong? [*She pauses and looks at* MOM.] Say, why are you still wearing your pajamas?

29 **MOM:** Today is Saturday, Linda. There is no school today.

[*Everyone looks at* LINDA *with a surprised, but also embarrassed expression.* LINDA *holds her head with an* "Oh, no!" *expression. The lights fade to black.*]

The End

Text Evidence Questions

1. Why doesn't Linda want to sleep in?

_____

_____

Text Evidence:

_____

_____

2. How would you describe the personality of Linda's sock Righty?

_____

_____

Text Evidence:

_____

_____

3. What household object do you think Boop is?

_____

_____

Text Evidence:

_____

_____

4. How much time has passed between Linda waking up and the end of the scene?

_____

_____

Text Evidence:

_____

_____

_____

MY STAR READER • GRADE 4 • ©2016 BENCHMARK EDUCATION COMPANY, LLC

Assessment Practice Questions

1. Based on the passage what inferences can you make about Linda's character? Support your answer using examples from the text.

_____

_____

_____

_____

_____

2. Use the stage directions at the beginning of the play to fill out the diagram below. Use these labels: Linda's bedroom; kitchen; hallway

Left   **Right**

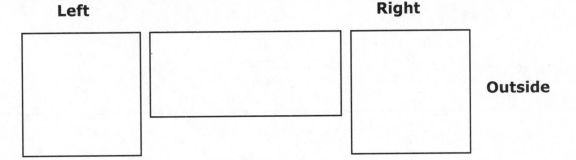

Outside

3. Choose the **best** summary of the passage.

   A. Linda wakes up at 7:00 a.m. because she does not want to be late for school. Linda gets ready, but her right sock makes her chase him. Linda falls back asleep.

   B. Linda's alarm clock, Boop, reminds Linda that she has been late to school every day that week.

   C. Linda tries to get ready for school in time. She cannot turn off her alarm. She cannot find her right sock. It is now past 7:15 a.m.

   D. Linda chases her socks.

Drama

Writing

The story "Heidi" uses several structural elements of a drama. Suppose you had to describe what a drama is to someone who had never heard of one before. Write a paragraph about "Heidi" to point out structural elements of a drama. Use the graphic organizer to record text evidence about the elements you will write about. Write your paragraph on the lines.

Structural Element of Drama	Text Evidence

_____

_____

_____

_____

_____

_____

Digging Deeper to Understand Text Structure

Answer the questions about "Heidi" to test your knowledge of the structural elements of dramatic literature.

1. What is the setting of "Heidi"?

_____

_____

2. Who are the characters in "Heidi"?

_____

_____

3. Which character is from Heidi's hometown in Switzerland?

_____

_____

4. Which stage direction explains how Heidi tells Grandmama how she knew she could never learn to read?

_____

_____

5. According to the stage directions, what happens right after Heidi's chin starts to quiver as she is talking to Grandmama?

_____

_____

6. What is the last dialogue of the drama?

_____

_____

Opinion Texts

What is an opinion text?

An opinion text is a written opinion that states an opinion on a specific topic. The writer needs to support his or her opinion with reasons based on facts, examples, and details. The text may be written as a letter addressed to a particular person or persons, or as an essay to be published.

What is the purpose of opinion texts?

In an opinion piece, the writer expresses an opinion about a topic he or she is passionate about. Often, the writer wants to persuade others to take his or her position on a particular issue. The writer's opinion may take the form of a "pro" or "con" (for or against) position.

How do you read an opinion text?

At the beginning, the writer introduces the topic and states an opinion. Look for the reasons that support the opinion. As you read, note the use of linking words that connect the opinions with the reasons behind them. Pay attention to the concluding statement or section that summarizes the opinion in a forceful way.

Who writes opinion texts?

People who write opinion texts clearly state an opinion on a topic. They know how to hook the reader with a strong beginning. When they list the reasons for the opinion, they often provide evidence from other sources that support each reason.

MY STAR READER • GRADE 4 • ©2016 BENCHMARK EDUCATION COMPANY, LLC

It has an organizational structure that clearly lists reasons for the opinion.

The text has a strong beginning that "hooks" the reader and clearly states an opinion.

It provides evidence from other sources that support each reason.

Features of an Opinion Text

It uses linking words to connect the opinions with the reasons behind them.

The text provides a concluding statement or section that summarizes the opinion in a powerful way.

Basketball
Is an Exciting Sport

Remember to highlight important information!

1   I have played both baseball and soccer, but when I tried basketball, I knew I had found the best sport of all. I think a sport should be fun as well as good for your body and mind. Also, you should be able to play on your own or with friends. And, you should only need to use simple equipment. Basketball easily meets all of these conditions.

2   First of all, to play basketball all you really need is a hoop and a basketball. You can play in your backyard or in your driveway. Plus, it's a sport you can play all year round, indoors or outdoors.

3   You can easily pass the time shooting hoops by yourself, or you can play with your friends or a team, five on five, to increase the fun and the challenge. Unlike other sports, all players on a team get the ball often. Players on a team get to play both offense and defense, so they are always doing different things. As a team player, you get to practice different skills.

4   Finally, basketball helps you build muscle, endurance, and quick reflexes. So basketball is not only fun, it's good for you.

5   Overall, the thing I like the most is that basketball is a really fast and exciting sport. You are never bored. Everyone should give basketball a try.

Swimming
Is the Best Sport

1   I pretty much like all sports, but if you ask me what my favorite sport is, I have an easy answer. It's the sport of Michael Phelps, the greatest swimmer ever, and one of the best athletes in history! Let me tell you why swimming is the best sport.

2   First of all, there is much more water than land on our planet, so we should all be able to swim. Swimming is a skill that you can use in a swimming pool, but also in lakes, rivers, and the ocean.

3   Secondly, have you ever seen a fish, dolphin, or whale get tired? Not really, right? Well, that's because they are swimmers! Swimming makes your heart and lungs strong. That means you will have more endurance, so you won't get tired easily. You will also be healthier. You know what else gets big and strong? Your muscles and your back become strong like a superhero's.

4   Swimming also helps me relax. When I feel nervous about a problem, some homework, or a test, swimming helps me calm down.

5   Finally, joining a swim club can help you make lots of new friends.

6   Swimming is a sport that makes you strong and confident, and it is so much fun to swim! These are the reasons why it is the best sport ever.

Opinion Texts

Find Text Evidence to Determine Cause and Effect

Causes/Reasons

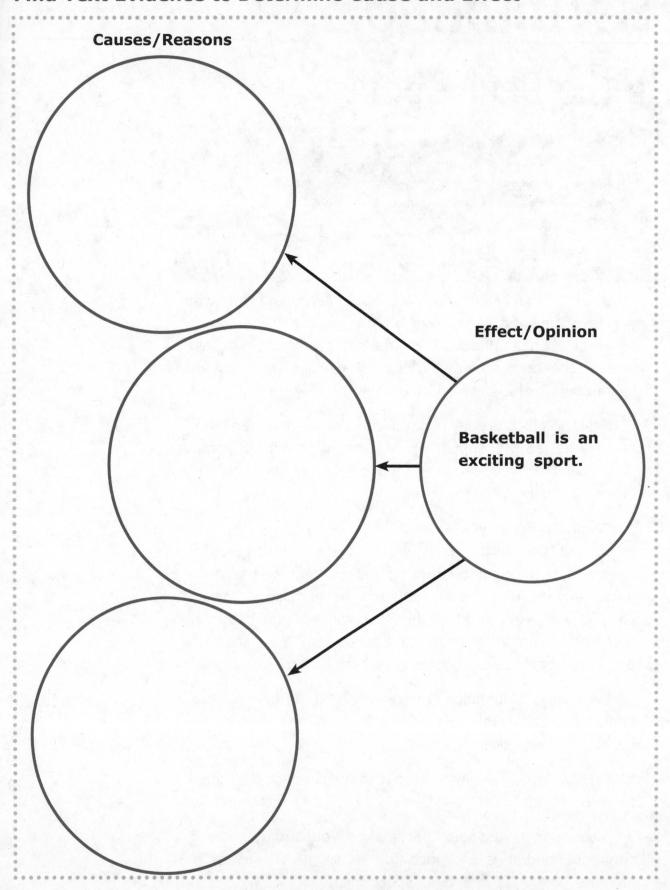

Effect/Opinion

Basketball is an exciting sport.

Find Text Evidence to Summarize the Text

Main Ideas

Summary

MY STAR READER • GRADE 4 • ©2016 BENCHMARK EDUCATION COMPANY, LLC

Independent Workstation ★ 1

Text Evidence Questions

1. How can you play basketball with other people?

_____

Text Evidence:

_____

2. Why are you always doing different things when you play on a basketball team?

_____

Text Evidence:

_____

_____

3. How do basketball and swimming help your body?

_____

Text Evidence:

_____

_____

_____

4. How can you make friends through swimming, according to the author of the second passage?

_____

Text Evidence:

_____

_____

Assessment Practice Questions

1. Which sentence **best** describes how swimming improves your endurance?

   A. It makes you faster.

   B. It makes your heart and lungs strong.

   C. It helps you relax.

   D. It helps you make lots of friends.

2. **Part A**

   In "Basketball Is an Exciting Sport," what idea from paragraph 1 is **best** supported by paragraph 4?

   A. A sport should be fun.

   B. You should be able to play on your own or with friends.

   C. A sport should use simple equipment.

   D. A sport should be good for your body and mind.

2. **Part B**

   What sentences from the passage **best** support your answer in part A?

   _____

   _____

   _____

Opinion Texts

Babe Ruth:

Baseball's Greatest Player

Highlight important information!

1   George Herman Ruth Jr. was born in 1895 in Baltimore, Maryland. He learned to play baseball when he was seven years old. He learned to hit, pitch, and catch a baseball.

2   Ruth always was an excellent player. When he was only nineteen years old, a baseball team hired him. He was the youngest player. His teammates called him "Babe." That is how he got his nickname.

3   Babe Ruth began as a pitcher. He played with the Boston Red Sox. He was the best batter on the team. Then Ruth played with the New York Yankees as an outfielder. Even though he was an outfielder, he was powerful at bat and skillful at catching the ball. In fact, his batting was amazing. Babe Ruth helped the New York Yankees to win four World Series titles.

4   Ruth played for twenty-one years. He retired in 1935 when he was forty years old. He had fifty-six Major League Baseball records.

5   Babe Ruth made the game of baseball fun and popular. He is perhaps the greatest baseball player in history.

Michael Jordan:

The Best Basketball Player of All Time

Notes:

1   Michael Jordan was born in Brooklyn, New York, in 1963. He loved playing basketball, and he was very good at it. When he was thirteen, his dad made him a basketball court. His neighbors gathered on weekends to play together.

2   In 1981, Jordan joined the basketball team at the University of North Carolina. One year later, he was named the best player in the country. He played in the Olympics two times. He played in the Los Angeles 1984 Olympic Games, and in the 1992 Barcelona Olympic Games. Michael won the gold medal both times.

3   In 1984, the Chicago Bulls selected Jordan to play for their team. He won six NBA championships, and scored the most points in the NBA in ten different seasons. Michael averaged 32 points per game, an NBA record. He was also named MVP many times.

4   I think he is the best basketball player ever. On the court, he was great because of his speed and intelligence. Off the court, he was great because of his humbleness.

5   He retired from basketball in 1999, but he will always be remembered by everyone.

Babe Ruth:

Baseball's Greatest Player

Highlight important information!

1   George Herman Ruth Jr. was born in 1895 in Baltimore, Maryland. When he turned seven, he learned to hit, pitch, and catch a baseball.

2   Ruth became an excellent player. He was only nineteen when a professional baseball team hired him. Since he was the youngest player, his teammates called him "Babe." That is how Babe Ruth got his nickname.

3   Ruth was a very good pitcher, and played the position with the Boston Red Sox. But he was also the best batter on the team. In 1920, Ruth began playing for the New York Yankees as an outfielder. Though he was an outfielder, Ruth was powerful with the bat and skillful at catching the ball. He combined a high batting average with a powerful swing, and hit hundreds of home runs. In fact, Babe Ruth helped the New York Yankees win four World Series titles.

4   Babe Ruth's baseball career lasted twenty-one years. He retired in 1935 and held fifty-six Major League Baseball records.

5   Babe Ruth made the game of baseball enjoyable and popular. After almost eighty years, he is still one of the greatest baseball players in history.

Michael Jordan:

The Best Basketball Player of All Time

Notes:

1   Michael Jordan was born in Brooklyn, New York, in 1963. He loved playing basketball. When Jordan was thirteen, his dad built him a basketball court. His neighbors gathered to play basketball together.

2   In 1981, Jordan joined the basketball team at the University of North Carolina. A year later, he won the NCAA MVP award. He played for the U.S. Olympic team in 1984 in Los Angeles, and again in Barcelona in 1992. The United States won the gold medal both years.

3   Jordan was drafted by the Chicago Bulls in 1984. He won six NBA championships for the Bulls, the NBA scoring title at the end of ten different seasons, and averaged 32 points per game—an NBA record. Jordan won the MVP award several times.

4   I think he is the best basketball player ever. On the court, he was great because of his speed and agility. Off the court, he was known for his humbleness.

5   In 1999, Michael Jordan retired from basketball. However, he will always be remembered as the greatest player of all time.

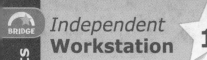

Independent Workstation 1

Text Evidence Questions

1. Why was Babe Ruth's nickname "Babe"?

_____

_____

Text Evidence:

_____

_____

2. What were Babe Ruth's strengths when he played for the New York Yankees?

_____

_____

Text Evidence:

_____

_____

3. Was Michael Jordan successful in the Olympics? How do you know?

_____

_____

Text Evidence:

_____

_____

4. What were Michael Jordan's traits as a player and as a person?

_____

_____

Text Evidence:

_____

_____

MY STAR READER • GRADE 4 • ©2016 BENCHMARK EDUCATION COMPANY, LLC

Assessment Practice Questions

1. **Part A**

Which sentence draws the **best** conclusion about Michael Jordan's years with the Chicago Bulls?

A. Michael Jordan was very successful when he played for the Chicago Bulls.

B. Michael Jordan started to play for the Chicago Bulls in 1984.

C. Michael Jordan chose the Olympic team over the Chicago Bulls.

D. Michael Jordan was not very good when he played for the Chicago Bulls.

1. **Part B**

Which statement from the text **best** supports your answer in part A?

A. "When he was thirteen, his father made him a basketball court."

B. "In 1981, he joined the basketball team at the University of North Carolina."

C. "He won six NBA championships, and scored the most points in the NBA in ten different seasons."

D. "On the court, he was great because of his speed and intelligence. Off the court, he was great because of his humbleness."

_____

2. Why was Babe Ruth "the greatest baseball player in history"? Use examples from the passage to support your answer.

_____

_____

_____

Opinion Texts

Writing

You have read about the similarities and differences between basketball and swimming. Use the chart to compare the important aspects of each sport. In the third column, choose a third sport and write some facts about it. Finally, use the lines below to write a short text in which you express which sport you like best and why.

Basketball	Swimming	

_____

_____

_____

_____

_____

_____

_____

Vocabulary

Antonyms are words that mean opposite things, such as *happy* and *sad,* or *quickly* and *slowly*.

1. Look back at the passages "Basketball Is an Exciting Sport" and "Swimming Is the Best Sport."

2. Find words that are antonyms of the words that appear in the chart.

3. Write the words in the chart below.

4. Choose four pairs of antonyms, and for each pair write one sentence that includes both words.

Word	Antonym
worst	
bad	
never	
less	
weak	
sicker	
relaxed	

_____

_____

_____

_____

_____

_____

FAIRY TALES

What is a fairy tale?

A fairy tale is a make-believe story about long ago and often starts with the words "Once upon a time." A fairy tale usually has characters who are good, characters who are evil, and characters with magical powers. Many fairy tales include kings, queens, princes, and princesses. Some have imaginary creatures, such as dragons, fairies, giants, and ogres.

What is the purpose of a fairy tale?

In a fairy tale, the storyteller often teaches a lesson. Fairy tales make people feel good at the end, since they almost always live "happily ever after."

How do you read a fairy tale?

First, figure out who the good and bad characters are. Then try to predict how the good characters will be rewarded and how the evil characters will be punished. Finally, be prepared for some magical surprises!

Who invented fairy tales?

People around the world told fairy tales for hundreds of years before the first written records were made. There are many similarities between fairy tales from different cultures. For example, Cinderella stories come from Egypt, Iceland, China, England, and dozens of other countries. By comparing the stories, we can learn about the places, history, and values that were important to each group of people.

MY STAR READER • GRADE 4 • ©2016 BENCHMARK EDUCATION COMPANY, LLC

The tale is a type of fantasy, often about royalty.

One character is helped by another.

The tale has a happy ending.

Features of a Fairy Tale

Often, people appear or events happen three times.

The tale often features fantastic or magical creatures; some animals and objects can talk.

A helper or a "bad guy" may have magical powers.

My Star Reader • Grade 4 • ©2016 Benchmark Education Company, LLC

A Golden Riddle

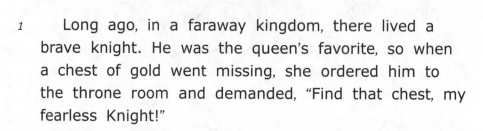

Remember to jot down your thinking!

1   Long ago, in a faraway kingdom, there lived a brave knight. He was the queen's favorite, so when a chest of gold went missing, she ordered him to the throne room and demanded, "Find that chest, my fearless Knight!"

2   Atop a high mountain, in a dark cave, the knight discovered the chest, a huge dragon curled around it. The knight stood boldly before the fearsome beast as it announced, "I know why you have come to my lair—you want to steal my chest of gold!"

3   "That chest of gold belongs to the queen, not to you," the knight <u>retorted</u>.

4   "Finders keepers," rumbled the dragon. "But I am willing to make you a deal: I will give you back the gold if you can solve my riddle; but if you cannot, I get to keep the chest of gold."

5   "Speak your riddle then."

6   The dragon smiled, showing all of his sharp teeth,

and said, "What creature loves gold more than I do, but always leaves it behind?"

7   The knight was stumped; everyone knows that dragons love gold more than any person or any thing. He could not come up with an answer.

8   The dragon taunted, "Do you give up?"

9   "Not yet! Give me a minute to think." The knight paced, trying to puzzle it out. He wandered over to the mouth of the cave and looked down at the castle far below. He was afraid he would fail the queen. The knight pictured her in the royal garden, surrounded by all of her yellow sunflowers.

10   "I know the answer!" exclaimed the knight. "The gold you speak of is the pollen of the sunflowers, and the creature that loves that gold more than you is the bee."

11   The dragon growled, fire escaping from his mouth. "Take the chest, Knight. You have won."

Notes:

Fairy Tales

Find Text Evidence to Identify Theme

Theme	Text Evidence

My Star Reader • Grade 4 • ©2016 Benchmark Education Company, LLC

Find Text Evidence to Summarize Main Events

Main Event	Text Evidence:
How Main Event Affects Story	**Text Evidence:**

Text Evidence Questions

1. Which detail in the passage suggests that the knight wished to please the queen?

_____

Text Evidence:

_____

_____

2. The purpose of the selection is to —

_____

Text Evidence:

_____

_____

_____

3. The dragon gives the knight a riddle in hopes that the dragon can —

_____

Text Evidence:

_____

_____

_____

4. The dragon is a trickster. Explain the actions of other tricksters you have read about.

_____

_____

Text Evidence:

_____

_____

Assessment Practice Questions

1. **Part A**

   What does the word <u>retorted</u> in paragraph 3 mean?

   A. verb, "to answer back"

   B. noun, "a clever remark"

   C. noun, "a machine that breaks substances up using heat"

   D. adjective, "cunning"

1. **Part B**

   Which reason **best** supports your answer to part A?

   A. There is a riddle involved.

   B. The dragon knows the knight will steal the gold back.

   C. The knight is replying to dragon's remark.

   D. The dragon has said something to the knight.

2. How do you think the story would be different if the dragon is telling the story? Why?

   _____

   _____

   _____

   _____

The Ugly Duckling

Highlight important information!

1   Once upon a time, down on an old farm, there lived a family of ducks. Mother Duck had been sitting on a clutch of five new eggs for quite some time.

2   One morning, four of the eggs hatched. Out popped four chirping ducklings. They were yellow and fuzzy and cute. But there still was one egg left in the nest, and it didn't look like the others.

3   Why wasn't the big, gray egg hatching? Then little pecking sounds came from within the egg.

4   *CLICK! CLICK! CLICK!*

5   Soon a gray beak poked through the shell. Out came a gray wing. Eventually the gray duckling was out of his egg.

6   "You're ugly," said one of the ducklings.

7   All of the ducklings grew quickly, and the yellow ones stayed yellow and the gray one stayed gray. The gray duckling ate a lot more than the yellow ones. He grew much bigger and was chubbier than his brothers.

8   At night, Mother Duck would shake her head at Father Duck.

9   "I can't understand how this ugly duckling can be one of ours," she said, shaking her head.

10   The gray duckling knew he was not like the others. As the days went by, the gray duckling became more and more unhappy.

Notes:

11   His brothers didn't want to be seen with him. So they didn't include him in farmyard play. All the other farmyard animals laughed at him, too. The ugly duckling was sad and lonely.

12   One day at sunrise, the ugly duckling ran away from home. As he walked through the forest, he stopped to talk to other birds.

13   "Do you know any ducklings that look like me?" he asked. But all of the birds turned up their noses at him.

14   Winter came and the water in the riverbed froze. The lonely duckling looked for food in the snow.

15   A kindly farmer saw the ugly duckling freezing on the ground. He picked up the duckling and took him home.

16   "This little thing is frozen," he said. "I'll take him home for my children to look after."

17   The duckling spent a pleasant winter with the kind farmer. By springtime, the gray duckling was full grown. So the farmer took him to the river to set him free. That was when the duckling saw his reflection in the water.

18   He saw a beautiful bird with a long, long neck.

19   "Who is that?" he asked himself. "What a handsome bird!"

20   A flight of swans glided onto the river. He looked at his reflection again. He suddenly realized he was one of their kind! He was a swan, just like them!

21   The swans became friends with the ugly duckling, who was no longer ugly or a duckling. He had found his true family. And he lived happily ever after!

The Ugly Duckling

Remember to jot down your thinking! →

1   Once upon a time, down on an old farm, there lived a family of ducks. Mother Duck had been sitting on a clutch of five new eggs for what seemed like forever.

2   One spring morning, four of the eggs hatched. Out popped four chirping ducklings, yellow and fuzzy and as cute as can be. But there still was one egg left in the nest. This last egg just didn't look like the others. It was big and gray and not very cute.

3   Why wasn't the big, gray egg hatching? Suddenly little pecking sounds came from within the egg.

4   *CLICK! CLICK! CLICK!*

5   A gray beak poked through the gray shell, and out came a gray wing. Eventually the gray duckling broke free from his gray egg.

6   "You're ugly," said one of his siblings.

7   All of the ducklings grew quickly, and the yellow ones stayed yellow and the gray one stayed gray. The gray duckling ate a lot more than the yellow ones, so he grew much bigger and was chubbier than his siblings.

8   At night, Mother Duck would shake her head at Father Duck.

9   "I can't understand how this ugly duckling can be one of ours," she cried.

10   The gray duckling knew he was not like the others, so as the days went by, he became more and more unhappy.

11   His siblings didn't want to be seen with him, so they didn't include him in farmyard play. All the other farmyard

Notes:

animals laughed at him, too. Oh, how sad and lonely the ugly duckling was!

12   One day at sunrise, the ugly duckling ran away from home. On his way through the forest, he stopped to talk to other birds.

13   "Do you know any ducklings that look like me?" he asked. But all of the birds turned up their noses at him.

14   Winter came and froze the water in the riverbed, forcing the lonely duckling to look for food in the snow.

15   One day a kindly farmer saw the ugly duckling freezing on the ground. He picked up the duckling and took him home.

16   "This little thing is frozen," he said. "My children will look after him well."

17   The duckling spent a pleasant winter with the kind farmer. By the springtime thaw, the gray duckling was full grown, so the farmer took him to the river to set him free. It was then that the duckling peered into the water.

18   He saw a beautiful bird with a long, long neck.

19   "Who is that?" he asked himself. "What a handsome bird!"

20   A flight of swans glided onto the river, and he looked at his reflection again. He suddenly realized he was one of their kind! He was a swan, just like them!

21   The swans became friends with the ugly duckling, who was no longer ugly or a duckling. He had found his true family. And he lived happily ever after!

Independent
Workstation **1**

Text Evidence Questions

1. Why is the Ugly Duckling considered "ugly"?

_____

_____

Text Evidence:

_____

_____

2. Why did the Ugly Duckling leave his duck family?

_____

_____

Text Evidence:

_____

_____

3. Is there a particular character telling this story? If so, who? If not, how do you know?

_____

_____

Text Evidence:

_____

_____

4. Why is the Ugly Duckling upset about being different?

_____

_____

Text Evidence:

_____

_____

My Star Reader • Grade 4 • ©2016 Benchmark Education Company, LLC

Assessment Practice Questions

1. What is the theme of the story?

    A. You should never give up on finding kind people you can be happy with.

    B. Friendship is more important than money.

    C. You should not do dangerous things to impress others.

    D. When people lie a lot, other people don't trust them.

2. Which words **best** describe how the ugly duckling felt when he ran away from home?

    A. scared and angry

    B. happy and excited

    C. sad and alone

    D. confused and lost

3. Why didn't the ugly duckling's brothers want to be seen with him? Use evidence from the text to support your answer.

    _____

    _____

    _____

    _____

    _____

Writing

In "A Golden Riddle," the dragon does not want to let the knight return the gold to the queen. How would you describe the relationship between the dragon and the knight at the beginning of the story? Then what happens to change the way the dragon feels?

Complete the chart. Then write a paragraph to explain your answer on the lines below.

Character Actions and Changes	Text Evidence

_____

_____

_____

_____

_____

_____

Read Across Texts

Use the chart to compare and contrast features of the folktale from page 22, "The Affair of the Hippopotamus and the Tortoise," with the fairy tale "A Golden Riddle" on page 164. On the lines describe how the theme of the folktale and the fairy tale are different from each other.

	"The Affair of the Hippopotamus and the Tortoise"	"A Golden Riddle"
Main Characters		
Setting		
Kinds of Events		
Outcome		

_____

_____

_____

Informational Texts: *Science*

What is an informational text?

An informational text is a nonfiction text that presents information in an accurate and organized way. It is often about a single subject, such as animal behavior, weather, or a scientific discovery.

What is the purpose of informational texts?

Informational texts have one main purpose: to inform. The best informational writing pulls readers in and makes them want to keep reading and to know more about the topic.

How do you read an informational text?

Look for facts and the details that support them. Read critically to make sure conclusions make sense. Ask yourself: *What is something new I learned from this text? What more do I want to know about it? What conclusion of my own can I draw from what I have read?*

Who writes informational texts?

Writers who know their topic well write good informational texts. They do this by becoming mini-experts on the subject they are writing about. They make sure that they support the information in their work with scientific data, graphics, and expert evidence. They use primary sources, like photographs.

The text has a strong beginning that "hooks" the reader.

The information is accurate, and the facts have been checked.

The text has a strong ending that keeps readers thinking.

Features of an Informational Text: *Science*

The text uses primary sources when appropriate.

The text has a logical organization of major concepts.

The information includes graphics that support the text.

My Star Reader • Grade 4 • ©2016 Benchmark Education Company, LLC

Our Friend the Bat

Remember to highlight important information! →

1 Bats are among the world's most interesting and amazing creatures. There are more than 1,000 different species of bats in the world. These range from large bats that measure almost 6 feet from wing to wing, to tiny bats that are no bigger than your finger.

2 Bats can live alone or in groups. A group of bats living together is called a colony. Bats have many different habitats; they can live in decaying trees, in caves, and even under bridges. Some people put up special houses for bats.

3 The diet of a bat is varied, ranging from insects to fruit to small animals such as mice and birds. Most of the bats that live in the United States and Canada eat insects, like beetles, flies, and gnats. In fact, a single bat can eat 2,000 to 6,000 insects in one night!

Notes:

4   Many people are frightened of bats, but unnecessarily so. They believe that bats will attack humans and get stuck in their hair. However, bats are not <u>vicious</u>, and they rarely bother people.

5   Bats can actually help us in many ways. For instance, they aid farmers by eating insects that destroy crops. Bats also keep mosquito populations down. Bats are pollinators, too; they carry pollen from one plant to another to help plants disperse their seeds and reproduce. In rain forests, bats help new plant life begin by spreading the seeds of plants or trees that have been cut down and burned. This helps plant life continue to flourish.

6   Today many people recognize that bats are an important part of a healthy environment and that it is crucial to keep these winged mammals protected and safe.

Find Text Evidence to Distinguish Fact from Opinion

Fact	Opinion

Find Text Evidence to Summarize the Text

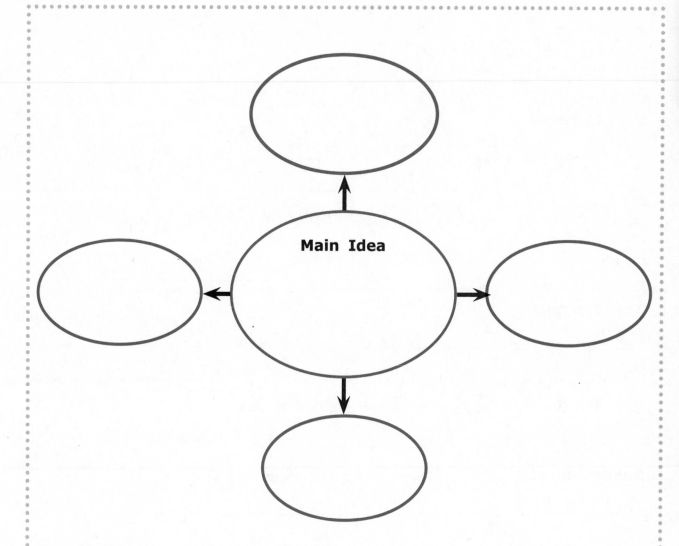

Main Idea

Summary

_____

_____

_____

_____

_____

_____

_____

Text Evidence Questions

1. What is paragraph 3 mainly about?

_____

Text Evidence:

_____

_____

2. Which detail from the passage suggests that bats easily adjust to different situations?

_____

Text Evidence:

_____

_____

3. What should you tell someone who is afraid of bats?

_____

Text Evidence:

_____

_____

4. Why does the author include paragraph 5 in the selection?

_____

_____

Text Evidence:

_____

_____

_____

Assessment Practice Questions

1. Reread this sentence from paragraph 4:

   Many people are frightened of bats, but unnecessarily so.

   Which reason **best** explains why this statement is an opinion?

   A. This statement is a fact, not an opinion.

   B. People who are afraid of bats may disagree.

   C. There is scientific evidence to support the statement.

   D. all of the above

2. What is paragraph 2 explaining?

   A. the diet of a bat

   B. how bats help the environment

   C. the habitat of bats

   D. how people feel about bats

3. Using a dictionary, look at the word <u>vicious</u> as it appears in paragraph 4. Then reread the sentence. How does the author show that the bat is not <u>vicious</u>?

   _____

   _____

   _____

   _____

Why Is the Sky Blue?

Highlight important information!

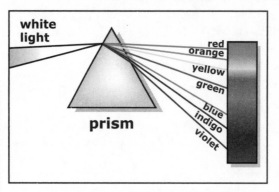

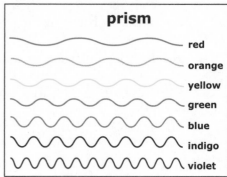

1   The sky is blue. Have you ever wondered why? Other smart people have too. It took a long time to figure out why the sky is blue.

2   The <u>light</u> from the sun looks white. But the light is really made up of the colors of the rainbow.

3   A prism is a specially shaped crystal. You can see all of light's colors when it shines through a prism.

4   Light energy travels in waves like ocean water. Some light travels in short, choppy waves. Other light travels in long, lazy waves. Blue light waves are shorter than red light waves.

5   All light travels in a straight line. That is, unless something:
 • reflects it (like a mirror);
 • bends it (like a prism);
 • or scatters it.

6   Sunlight is scattered when it hits Earth's atmosphere. Gases and particles in the air scatter the light. Blue light is scattered more than other colors because it travels in shorter, smaller waves. This is why the sky looks blue most of the time.

Notes:

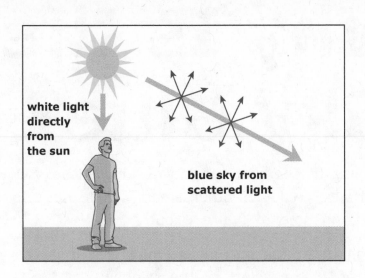

white light
directly
from
the sun

blue sky from
scattered light

7   The sky looks lighter blue or white closer to the horizon. The sunlight reaching us from low in the sky passes through more air than the sunlight above us. The air molecules scatter the blue light many times in many directions. Also, the surface of Earth reflects and scatters light. All this scattering mixes the colors together so we see more white and less blue.

What Makes a Red Sunset?

8   Light passes through more of the atmosphere when the sun sets. Even more blue light scatters. This makes the sky look red and yellow.

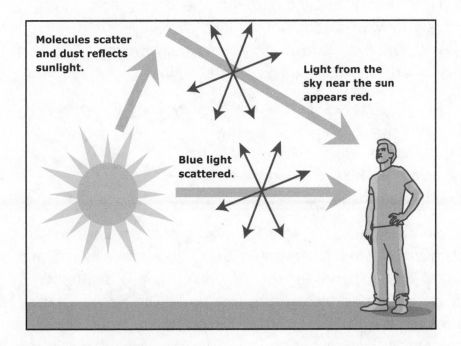

Molecules scatter
and dust reflects
sunlight.

Light from the
sky near the sun
appears red.

Blue light
scattered.

Remember to jot down your thinking!

Why Is the Sky Blue?

1   It is easy to see that the sky is blue. Have you ever wondered why? A lot of other smart people have too. And it took a long time to figure it out!

2   The <u>light</u> from the sun looks white. But it is really made up of all the colors of the rainbow.

3   A prism is a specially shaped crystal. When white light shines through a prism, the light is separated into all its colors.

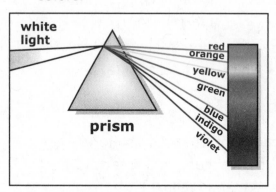
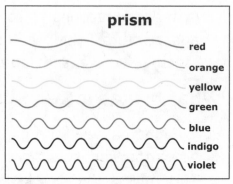

4   Like energy passing through the ocean, light energy travels in waves too. Some light travels in short, choppy waves. Other light travels in long, lazy waves. Blue light waves are shorter than red light waves.

5   All light travels in a straight line. That is, unless something:

- reflects it (like a mirror);
- bends it (like a prism);
- or scatters it.

6   So what scatters light? Sunlight reaches Earth's atmosphere and is scattered in all directions by all the gases and particles in the air. Blue light is scattered in all directions by the tiny molecules of air in Earth's atmosphere. Blue is scattered more than other colors because it travels as shorter, smaller waves. This is why we see a blue sky most of the time.

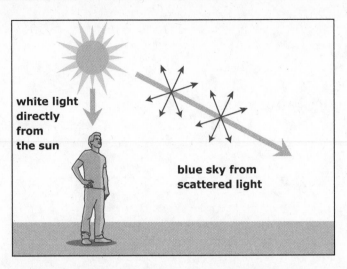

white light directly from the sun

blue sky from scattered light

7   Closer to the horizon, the sky fades to a lighter blue or white. The sunlight reaching us from low in the sky passes through even more air than the sunlight reaching us from overhead. As the sunlight passes through all this air, the air molecules scatter the blue light many times in many directions. Also, the surface of Earth reflects and scatters the light. All this scattering mixes the colors together again so we see more white and less blue.

What Makes a Red Sunset?

8   As the sun gets lower in the sky, its light passes through more of the atmosphere to reach us. Even more of the blue light is scattered. This allows the reds and yellows to pass straight through to our eyes.

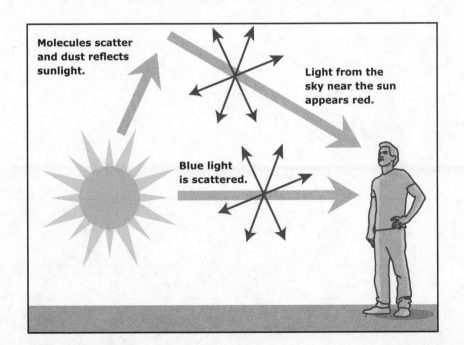

Molecules scatter and dust reflects sunlight.

Light from the sky near the sun appears red.

Blue light is scattered.

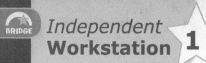

Informational Texts

Text Evidence Questions

1. What stops light from moving in a straight line?

_____

_____

Text Evidence:

_____

_____

2. Why does the sky look blue instead of red most of the time?

_____

_____

Text Evidence:

_____

_____

3. Why does the horizon look more white than blue?

_____

_____

Text Evidence:

_____

_____

4. What can prisms tell us about white light?

_____

_____

Text Evidence:

_____

_____

Assessment Practice Questions

1. The sky can look red, white, blue, and light blue. Sometimes, the sky can look pink when the sun is setting. Why might this be so? Use examples from the passage to support your answer.

_____

_____

_____

_____

2. **Part A**

   What definition **best** describes how <u>light</u> (first used in paragraph 2) is used in this passage?

   A. not heavy

   B. a lamp

   C. a flame or match

   D. what helps us see

2. **Part B**

   What sentence from the text **best** supports your answer to part A?

   A. "The light from the sun looks white."

   B. "The sky looks lighter blue or white closer to the horizon."

   C. "It took a long time to figure out why the sky is blue."

   D. "All light travels in a straight line."

Informational Texts

Writing

At the beginning of "Our Friend the Bat," the author states that bats are among the world's most interesting and amazing creatures. Use what you read in the text and what you know about other animals to draw an inference about this statement. Then explain the reason(s) behind that inference. Use the graphic organizer to help you organize your ideas before you write on the lines below.

What I Read	What I Know	Inference

_____

_____

_____

_____

_____

_____

Read Across the Texts

1. Use the chart to list ways "Our Friend the Bat" on page 180 is different from "The Silk Road" on page 108.

	Our Friend the Bat	**The Silk Road**
Genre		
Main Idea		
Supporting Detail		
Author's Purpose		

2. In what way are the two texts alike?

_____

_____

_____

_____

_____

Poetry

What is a poem?

_____

_____

_____

What is the purpose of a poem?

_____

_____

_____

_____

How do you read a poem?

_____

_____

_____

_____

Who invented poems?

_____

_____

_____

_____

Features of a Poem

It is often short.

Uses imagery to capture a moment, tell a story, or convey an emotion.

It has rhythm.

Lines can be a word, a phrase, or a full sentence.

Lines can be rhymed or unrhymed.

Lines can be grouped to form a stanza.

MY STAR READER • GRADE 4 • ©2016 BENCHMARK EDUCATION COMPANY, LLC

Remember to take notes! →

The Flower's Lesson

by Louisa May Alcott

"O sister," said the little rose bud, as she gazed
   at the sky,
"I wish that the Dew Elves, as they wander lightly by,
Would bring me a star; for they never grow dim,
The shining drops of dew the Elves bring each day
5 And place in my bosom, so soon pass away;
But a star would glitter brightly through the long
   summer hours,
And I should be fairer than all my sister flowers.
That were better far than the dew-drops that fall
On the high and the low, and come alike to all.
10 I would be fair and stately, with a bright star to shine
And give a queenly air to this crimson robe of mine."
And proudly she cried, "These fire-flies shall be
My jewels, since the stars can never come to me."
Just then a tiny dew-drop that hung o'er the dell
15 On the breast of the bud like a soft star fell
But impatiently she flung it away from her leaf,
And it fell on her mother like a tear of grief,
While she folded to her breast, with wilful pride,
A glittering fire-fly that hung by her side.
20 "Heed," said the mother rose, "daughter mine,
Why shouldst thou seek for beauty not thine?
O my foolish little bud, do listen to thy mother;
Care only for true beauty, and seek for no other.
There will be grief and trouble in that wilful little heart;
25 Unfold thy leaves, my daughter, and let the fly depart."
But the proud little bud would have her own will,

And folded the fire-fly more closely still;
Till the struggling insect tore open the vest
Of purple and green, that covered her breast.

30 When the sun came up, she saw with grief
The blooming of her sister bud leaf by leaf.
While she, once as fair and bright as the rest,
Hung her weary head down on her wounded breast.
Bright grew the sunshine, and the soft summer air

35 Was filled with the music of flowers singing there;
But faint grew the little bud with thirst and pain,
And longed for the cool dew; but now't was in vain.
Then bitterly she wept for her folly and pride,
As drooping she stood by her fair sister's side.

40 Then from the mother's breast, where it still lay hid,
Into the fading bud the dew-drop gently slid;
Stronger grew the little form, and happy tears fell,
As the dew did its silent work, and the bud grew
well,
While the gentle rose leaned, with motherly pride,

45 O'er the fair little ones that bloomed at her side.
Night came again, and the fire-flies flew;
But the bud let them pass, and drank of the dew.

Find Text Evidence to Summarize the Text

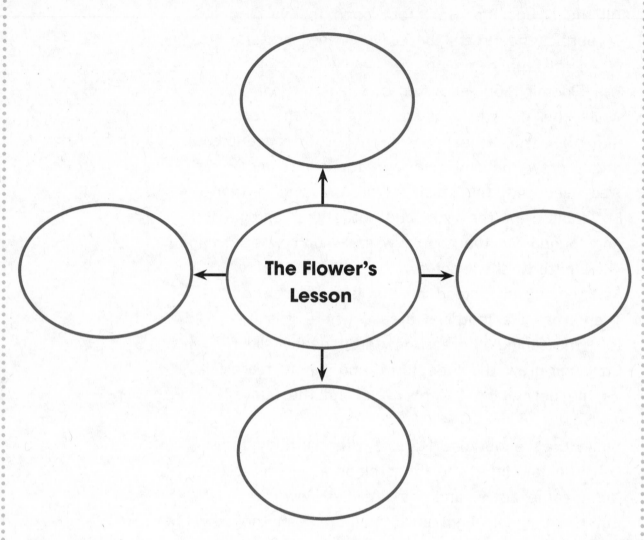

The Flower's Lesson

Summary

_____

_____

_____

_____

_____

_____

_____

Find Text Evidence to Analyze Sensory Language

Type of Sensory Language	Text Evidence	Meaning

Independent
Workstation 1

Text Evidence Questions

1. How can you tell "The Flower's Lesson" is a poem?

_____

Text Evidence:

_____

2. What is the theme of the poem?

_____

Text Evidence:

_____

_____

_____

_____

3. How does the young flower learn her lesson?

_____

Text Evidence:

_____

_____

_____

4. Why does the flower ignore the fire-fly at the end of the poem?

_____

_____

Text Evidence:

_____

_____

My Star Reader • Grade 4 • ©2016 Benchmark Education Company, LLC

Assessment Practice Questions

1. Part A

Using a dictionary, find the definition of the word <u>heed</u> found in line 20 of the poem. Which definition **best** fits the use of heed here?

A. ignore

B. pay attention

C. awareness

D. to feel happy

1. Part B

What context clue **best** supports your answer to part A?

A. A mother is speaking to her daughter.

B. A fire-fly is captured in the flower's petals.

C. The flower is willful.

D. The flower flung away a dew-drop.

_____

2. How do you know that this passage is a poem?

_____

_____

_____

_____

Snow Music

by Sheri Lynn Doyle

Highlight important information!

What's the sound
Of falling snow?
A sleeping swan
With head tucked low.

5 Ice cream dripping
Down a cone.
A polar bear
That swims alone.

Sugar dusting
10 Angel cakes.
Is that the sound
A snowfall makes?

Poetry

The Silver Bears

by Sheri Lynn Doyle

Remember
to take
notes!
→

I have two very special friends.
Their fur is silver, so it blends
with all the snow that Winter sends.

5 They ride the North Wind as it blows
from deep within the Land of Snows,
to nip your fingers, ears, and nose.

These friendly bears are very shy,
and blow the snow into the sky
so they can play and hide nearby.

Notes:

10 They storm your fort. He hops your sled.
She juggles snowballs overhead.
They dance and prance while you're in
bed.

On nights when you're just lying there,
15 and wind is howling everywhere,
don't get upset and don't despair—

It's probably just a silver bear!

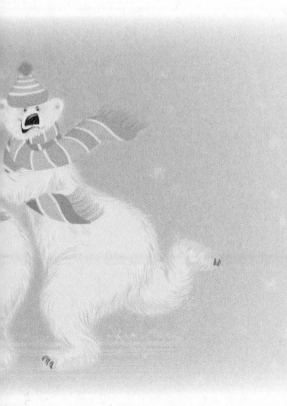

Text Evidence Questions

1. Does the speaker of the poem know what snowfall sounds like?

_____

_____

Text Evidence:

_____

_____

2. What images can be seen in this poem?

_____

_____

Text Evidence:

_____

_____

_____

3. Look at lines 7 and 8. This is your text evidence. *A polar bear / That swims alone.* What do these lines say about the sound of snowfall?

_____

_____

4. Look in the dictionary for the word *tranquil*. Does the speaker of the poem think snowfall is tranquil?

_____

_____

Text Evidence:

_____

_____

Assessment Practice Questions

1. Based on the poem, what word **best** describes the sound of snowfall?

   A. loud

   B. annoying

   C. soft

   D. silly

2. Which reasons **best** explain why the author started and ended the poem with a question? Choose all that apply.

   A. to ask the reader what snowfall sounds like

   B. so the speaker can answer the question in the poem

   C. to show that the speaker is wondering about the sound of snow

   D. to show that a snowfall can be described in many ways

3. Why do you think the title of the poem is "Snow Music" even though the poem does not discuss music directly?

   _____

   _____

   _____

   _____

Writing

Read the following lines from the poem.

> Bright grew the sunshine, and the soft summer air
> Was filled with the music of flowers singing there;

Write a paragraph about what you picture in your mind when you read these lines. Which words help you create that image? First complete the chart with the images you picture in your mind. Then write your paragraph on the lines below.

Word	Image

_____

_____

_____

_____

_____

_____

Digging Deeper into Rhyme

Part 1. Directions:

Find the words that rhyme in the lines from "The Flower's Lesson." Circle the rhyming words.

"O sister," said the little rose bud, as she gazed
    at the sky,
"I wish that the Dew Elves, as they wander lightly by,
Would bring me a star; for they never grow dim,
The shining drops of dew the Elves bring each day
5 And place in my bosom, so soon pass away;
But a star would glitter brightly through the long
    summer hours,
And I should be fairer than all my sister flowers.
That were better far than the dew-drops that fall
On the high and the low, and come alike to all.
10 I would be fair and stately, with a bright star to shine
And give a queenly air to this crimson robe of mine."

Part 2. Directions:

Write the pairs of rhyming words you circled from "The Flower's Lesson."

_____

_____

_____

_____

Informational Texts: *Science*

What is an informational text?

_____

_____

_____

_____

What is the purpose of informational texts?

_____

_____

_____

_____

How do you read an informational text?

_____

_____

_____

_____

Who writes informational texts?

_____

_____

_____

_____

The text has a strong beginning that "hooks" the reader.

The information is accurate, and the facts have been checked.

The text has a strong ending that keeps readers thinking.

Features of an Informational Text: *Science*

The text uses primary sources when appropriate.

The text has a logical organization of major concepts.

The information includes graphics that support the text.

Biodiesel

1   Biodiesel is a renewable fuel. It can be used instead of diesel fuel, which is made from petroleum. Biodiesel can be made from vegetable oils, animal fats, or greases. Most biodiesel today is made from soybean oil. Some is made from used oils or fats, including recycled restaurant grease.

2   Biodiesel is most often blended with small amounts of petroleum diesel. But it can also be used in pure form. Biodiesel can be used in regular diesel vehicles without making any changes to the engines. It can also be stored and transported using diesel tanks and trucks.

3   Using biodiesel to run car and small truck engines has just started to catch on, but it isn't a new idea. Before petroleum diesel fuel became popular, Rudolf Diesel, the inventor of the diesel engine in 1897, experimented with using vegetable oil as fuel.

Biodiesel as a Transportation Fuel

4   Most larger trucks, buses, and tractors in the United States use diesel fuel. But it is a nonrenewable fuel made from petroleum. Using biodiesel means that we use a little less petroleum. Biodiesel results in less pollution, too. Any vehicle that operates on diesel fuel can switch to biodiesel without changes to its engine. Some biodiesel blends are popular in the trucking industry because they can improve engine performance.

5   Biodiesel fuels are sensitive to cold weather. They may require a special antifreeze, just as petroleum diesel fuel does. But biodiesel has another plus. It acts like a detergent additive. It loosens and dissolves sediments that build up in storage tanks. Pure biodiesel fuel is a solvent. It may cause rubber and other parts to fail in older vehicles. But this problem does not occur with biodiesel blends.

Biodiesel Use

6   Because of environmental benefits and ease of use, biodiesel use in the United States has increased. It grew from about 10 million gallons in 2001 to 358 million gallons in 2007. Government programs and low taxes helped increase biodiesel use after that. By 2011, U.S. drivers were using 878 million gallons a year. And biodiesel was being exported to other countries, too.

7   Some regular cars and pickup trucks now run on biodiesel. But in this country, it is used mostly by fleet vehicles. These include school buses, snowplows, garbage trucks, mail trucks, and military vehicles. Some uses of biodiesel fuels are required by federal or state laws. There are fueling stations that sell biodiesel fuels to the public in nearly every state.

8   The table below shows the use of biodiesel around the world. More than half of the biodiesel used was sold in only five countries.

World Biodiesel Consumption, 2010

Biodiesel Consumption	Billion Gallons	Share of Total
World Total	5.36	
Germany	0.77	14%
Brazil	0.65	12%
France	0.61	11%
Italy	0.46	9%
Spain	0.40	7%
All Others	2.47	47%

Find Text Evidence to Understand Organization

Text Structure Paragraph 5	Text Evidence
Text Structure Paragraph 6	Text Evidence

Find Text Evidence to Summarize the Text

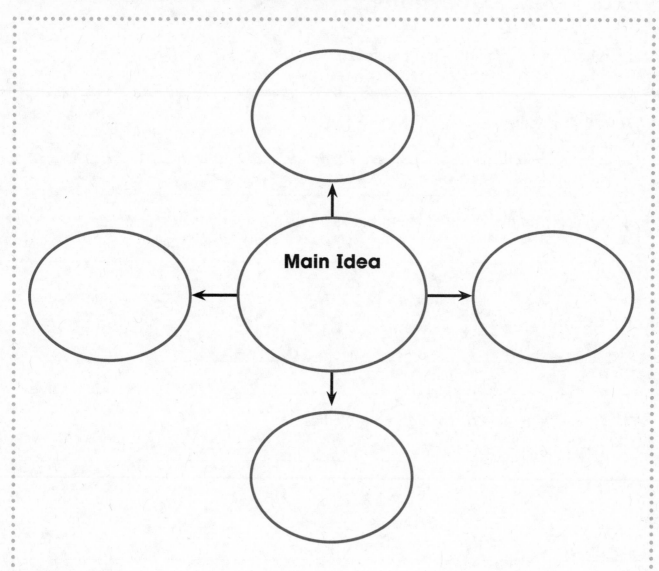

Main Idea

Summary

_____

_____

_____

_____

_____

_____

_____

Text Evidence Questions

1. What are benefits of using biodiesel?

_____

Text Evidence:

_____

_____

2. What is one drawback of using biodiesel fuel in your car or truck today?

_____

_____

Text Evidence:

_____

_____

3. Why is vegetable oil considered a biodiesel?

_____

Text Evidence:

_____

_____

_____

4. Why does the author include a chart instead of putting the information in the text?

_____

_____

Text Evidence:

_____

_____

Assessment Practice Questions

1. **Part A**

   In what paragraph can you **best** learn about what biodiesel is?

   A. Paragraph 4

   B. Paragraph 1

   C. Paragraph 8

   D. Paragraph 5

1. **Part B**

   What is the **best** summary of paragraph 1?

   A. Soybean oil is the best option for biodiesel.

   B. Biodiesel can come from recycled materials.

   C. Fats from vegetables, animals, and kitchen grease can be used as biodiesel.

   D. Biodiesel is not petroleum.

2. Do you think the United States should use more biodiesel? If so, why? Use the passage to support your answer.

   _____

   _____

   _____

   _____

   _____

The National Zoo

from the Smithsonian National Zoological Park

Highlight important information!

1   We are the Smithsonian National Zoological Park in Washington, D.C. We are also called the National Zoo. About 2,000 animals live here, like great apes, big cats, elephants, birds, reptiles, and many more! Learn more about our animals and the areas of the zoo.

Giant Pandas

2   First, visit the giant pandas. Giant pandas are black-and-white bears. They are from central China's mountain forests. As few as 1,600 giant pandas are still alive in the wild. More than 300 pandas live in zoos around the world. Most of these pandas are in China.

Birds

3   Next, visit the Bird House. Many birds live at the National Zoo. Birds are all over the zoo. Some are residents. Others are visitors.

Asian Elephants

4   Don't forget the Asian elephants! Thirty-two pickle barrels were donated to the zoo. The zoo's animal-care staff hung them up. The elephants bang on the barrels. The elephants smell and play with the barrels, too.

Notes:

Great Ape House

5 The great apes are next! During the summer, keepers at the zoo's Great Ape House put a few piles of sand in the gorillas' yard. The gorillas got shovels, about twenty sand buckets filled with ice, and beach towels. The animals had a lot of fun!

Reptile Discovery Center

6 Now go see the reptiles! The world has 8,240 different reptiles. Turtles, snakes, crocodiles, and lizards are all reptiles. They can be less than an inch long. They can weigh more than a ton! All reptiles have scales. Some scales are too small to see, though. Most reptiles lay eggs. A few give birth to live young.

Seals and Sea Lions

7 Then visit the seals and sea lions at the new American Trail exhibit. This exhibit features ten species from North America.

Great Cats

8 Next, go see the Great Cats exhibit. We have tigers and lions. Two lions each gave birth to a <u>litter</u> of cubs in 2010. Four cubs were born in August. Three cubs were born in September.

Kids' Farm

9 Lastly, visit the Kids' Farm. You can learn about alpacas, cows, donkeys, hogs, and goats!

The National Zoo

from the Smithsonian National Zoological Park

Highlight important information!

1 About 2,000 animals reside at the Smithsonian National Zoological Park, also called the National Zoo, in Washington, D.C. Our best-known residents are our giant pandas. The zoo is also home to great apes, big cats, elephants, birds, reptiles, and many more! Learn more about our animals and areas of the zoo.

Giant Pandas

2 Start your visit with the giant pandas. Giant pandas are black-and-white bears. As few as 1,600 giant pandas survive in the mountain forests of central China. More than 300 pandas live in zoos around the world. Most of these pandas are in China.

Birds

3 Next, visit the Bird House. The National Zoo is home to hundreds of birds. It's not surprising that birds are all over the zoo, as residents and visitors.

Asian Elephants

4 Don't forget the Asian elephants! The zoo recently got a donation of thirty-two pickle barrels. The zoo's animal-care staff hang up the welcome gifts. Then the elephants bang on the barrels, smell them, and play with them.

Great Ape House

5 The great apes are next! To celebrate summer, keepers at the zoo's Great Ape House had fun. They put a few piles of sand, shovels, and about twenty sand

Notes:

buckets filled with ice throughout the gorillas' yard. The gorillas were also given beach towels. These activities provide a lot of fun for the animals.

Reptile Discovery Center

6   Now go see the reptiles! The world has 8,240 different reptiles. Reptiles include turtles, snakes, crocodiles, and lizards. They can be as small as the dwarf gecko (less than an inch long). They can be as big as the saltwater crocodile. They can weigh more than a ton! All reptiles have scales, but some of those are too small to be seen. Most reptiles lay eggs, but a few give birth to live young.

Seals and Sea Lions

7   After that, visit the seals and sea lions at the National Zoo's wonderful new American Trail exhibit. This exhibit features ten species from North America.

Great Cats

8   Next, go see the big cats! The Great Cats exhibit has tigers and lions. In 2010, two lions each gave birth to a litter of cubs. Four cubs were born in August. Three cubs were born in September.

Kids' Farm

9   End your visit with animals you see at a farm. Learn about alpacas, cows, donkeys, hogs, and goats. If you come to the National Zoo, be sure to visit the Kids' Farm in person!

Text Evidence Questions

1. What is the purpose of the first paragraph?

_____

_____

Text Evidence:

_____

_____

2. How does being in the National Zoo benefit the giant pandas?

_____

Text Evidence:

_____

_____

3. In what paragraph can you learn about elephants?

_____

Text Evidence:

_____

4. What is the main idea of the section "Reptile Discovery Center"?

_____

_____

Text Evidence:

_____

_____

_____

MY STAR READER • GRADE 4 • ©2016 BENCHMARK EDUCATION COMPANY, LLC

Assessment Practice Questions

1. What did the zoo's keepers give to the gorillas?

   A. sunscreen, beach towels, sand, barrels

   B. sand, shovels, beach towels, barrels

   C. ice buckets, barrels, beach towels, sand

   D. sand, shovels, buckets with ice, beach towels

2. Imagine you are a tour guide at the National Zoo giving a tour to a large crowd. In your own words, how would you describe the zoo to the crowd before starting the tour? Use examples from the passage.

   _____

   _____

   _____

   _____

   _____

   _____

3. Which definition **best** describes the use of <u>litter</u> in paragraph 8 of this passage?

   A. a group of newborn cubs

   B. garbage

   C. to scatter objects

   D. a stretcher

Informational Texts

Writing

The text "Biodiesel Fuel" has a section called "Biodiesel Use" in which the author explains how biodiesel use is increasing around the world. Do you think biodiesel should be used in more countries? Why or why not? Reread the text and look for text evidence to answer the question. Use the chart to organize your ideas. Then write your opinion on the lines below.

Text Evidence	Text Evidence	Text Evidence

_____

_____

_____

_____

_____

_____

_____

Read Across the Texts

1. Use the Venn diagram to compare "Biodiesel" on page 212 to "The Silk Road" on page 108.

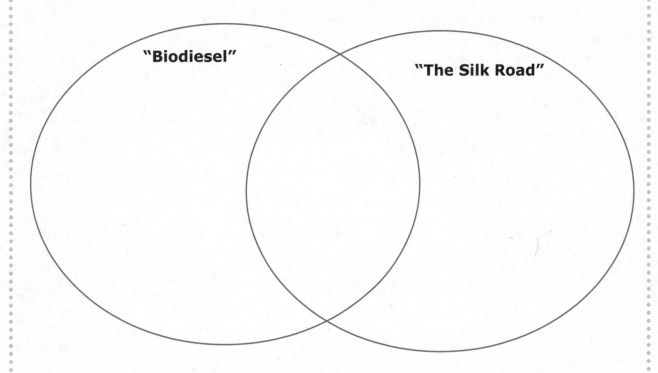

2. In what ways are "Biodiesel" and "The Silk Road" alike? How are they different?

Alike:

_____

_____

Different:

_____

_____

_____

_____

Notes: